De L

Tree Ink Art Credit To My Talented Friend Katerina Klvackov

The layout of this book is specifically arranged differently for a few reasons.

1) Regular book text is boring & tires the eyes. (IMO)
2) Our attention span is shorter - so let's get to the point & the many questions.
3) Texting & short bursts of information are more familiar these days - so, this book is written, as I would text a friend.
4) Not everyone is a reader or a good one at that!
   So why not accommodate to what is familiar?
5) This is NOT a chapter book

After all, this book is for the greatest good of all!
&, a lot of the **ALL** have not achieved diplomas, want to, or - found that having such - did not prepare them for this life experience.

But make no mistake - we all are so super smart - in so many ways... 
You may believe otherwise because ...
society decided one requires X, Y & Z to be "successful!" 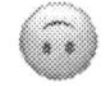
SO NOT TRUE!
It is up to you to decide who limits who ...
YOU LIMIT YOU - IF YOU SO CHOOSE!

The title of this book is a question that was Shared with me in the late 90's...
by **the lovely Barbara Preston,** who I spent some Bible Study time with. 
The original author of the question is Unknown!
This question - is something I have always come back to...
no matter where life has taken me.
Barbara appeared in my life - just weeks before my mothers passing!
& interestingly enough...
I do believe our first subject was around death...
We discussed our individual thoughts around death & mourning.
Barbara - then brought to light some scriptures to explore.

De L

Now, Here I Stand in **Appreciation** of all my life experiences -
(the good, the bad & the oh so ugly!)
I have learned so many things - so many lessons, in each & every experience.
There truly is a silver lining to every experience - if, you choose to see it!

Today, I stand tall in my truth, as I value myself -
in a way I once - never thought possible.
I tend to be full of common sensibles & so much more.
I believe that we all... really should learn how to value ourselves -
for the amazing true gem that we are

My hope is that this book helps you - travel **your** path, to standing tall -
tall in your **own truth** & be **successfully proud to be you**, because...
you my honey friend - you are worthy of getting to know
your authentic self & see your true value too

For those no longer in my life - whether it be your choice or mine...
Your actions or reactions - may have told me more about you & that
you did not or do not align with what is in my best interests -
nor mine yours.
It is - all very much ok & as it should be
Sometimes - we are only meant to be in each others life, for a reason
or a season - of fun, of joy, of growing & learning
This is life in the human experience - So let's value it!

I do wish everyone well on their own life path &...
I do believe - that this small creation can help impact positively - for those
who seek to make their personal connection - authentically theirs

I say it's time to align within - because you are worthy

Everyone deserves to experience forms of joy in the best way...
no matter their circumstances - true?
There is as much happiness as there is sadness,
with the stronger focus on the negative - sadly!

So - it is up to you to **Choose** - to see **the positive** -
Grab that lil slice of Joy Daily...
Appreciate it in the moment & watch that Positive expand.

Do you realize... it is a choice to allow the positive in -
as you sift & sort your choices?

Happiness can be as simple as...
discovering & appreciating the moments of joy on this journey to
THE DESIRED DESTINATION ❣

HAPPINESS IS THE JOURNEY -
NOT NECESSARILY THE DESTINATION!

Other Influences & experiences on this discovery of 'My WITHIN'
led me here owning "this is my Life" because of the choices I chose ...
are as follows:

'IMAGINE' by John Lennon
(One of our dads fave songs :-)
IMAGINE / Imagination
A powerful word & tool that can truly help one & all
through life's journey...
if one & all can ... stay completely & truly connected
with the imagination for their greatest good -
regardless of their surroundings!
I DO NOT OWN ANY RIGHTS TO THE FOLLOWING LYRICS
I WISH TO SHARE THE BEAUTY OF THEM
ONLY!

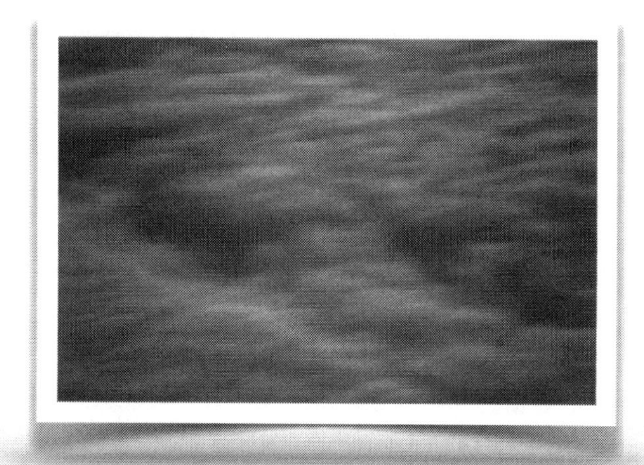

Imagine there's no heaven
It's easy if you try
No hell below us
Above us, only sky
Imagine all the people
Livin' for today
Ah
Imagine there's no countries
It isn't hard to do
Nothing to kill or die for
And no religion, too
Imagine all the people
Livin' life in peace
You
You may say I'm a dreamer
But I'm not the only one
I hope someday you'll join us
And the world will be as one
Imagine no possessions
I wonder if you can
No need for greed or hunger
A brotherhood of man
Imagine all the people
Sharing all the world
You
You may say I'm a dreamer
But I'm not the only one
I hope someday you'll join us
And the world will live as one

'SEARCH FOR THE HERO' by M People
(Our mams favorite song :-)
Your Hero is YOUR INNER YOU - waiting for you to Align ...
a Process only you can achieve for you -
through your choices!
Others can only guide you towards this process.
Your key (true love of self) is for you to find!
I DO NOT OWN ANY RIGHTS TO THE FOLLOWING LYRICS
I WISH TO SHARE THE BEAUTY OF THEM ONLY!

Sometimes the river flows but nothing breathes
A train arrives but never leaves, it's a shame
Oh, life like love that's walked out of the door
Of being rich or being poor, such a shame

But it's then, then that faith arrives
To make your feelings alive
And that's why, you should keep on aiming high
Just seek yourself and you will shine

You've got to search for the hero inside
yourself
Search for the secrets you hide
Search for the hero inside yourself
Until you find the key to your life

In this life, long and hard though it may seem
Live it as you'd live a dream, aim so high
Just keep the flame of truth burning bright
The missing treasure you must find
Mmm-mmm-mmm

Because you and only you alone
Can build a bridge across the stream
Weave your spell in life's rich tapestry
Your passport to a feeling supreme

You've got to search for the hero inside yourself
Search for the secrets you hide
Search for the hero inside yourself
Until you find the key to your life

You've got to search, inside yourself
Deep, deep down inside yourself, yeah
You've got to search, inside yourself

You've got to search for the hero inside yourself (ooh)
Search for the secrets you hide
Search for the hero inside yourself
Until you find the key to your life

Search for the hero inside yourself (oh yeah)
Search for the secrets you hide (all of the secrets you hide)
Search for the hero inside yourself (you'll find a hero)
Until you find the key to your life

You've got to search inside yourself
You've got to search

'TOP OF THE WORLD' by The Carpenters
(A favorite of mine! :-)
You deserve to be on top of your world!
I truly believe if you connect to your authentic self ...
then this song will have some feeling connection for you too!
I DO NOT OWN ANY RIGHTS TO THE FOLLOWING LYRICS
I DO WISH TO SHARE THE BEAUTY OF THEM ONLY!

Such a feelin's comin' over me
There is wonder in most every thing I see
Not a cloud in the sky, got the sun in my eyes
And I won't be surprised if it's a dream

Everything I want the world to be
Is now comin' true especially for me
And the reason is clear, it's because you are here
You're the nearest thing to heaven that I've seen

I'm on the top of the world lookin' down on creation
And the only explanation I can find
Is the love that I've found, ever since you've been around
Your love's put me at the top of the world

Something in the wind has learned my name
And it's tellin' me that things are not the same
In the leaves on the trees, and the touch of the breeze
There's a pleasing sense of happiness for me

There is only one wish on my mind
When this day is through I hope that I will find
That tomorrow will be, just the same for you and me
All I need will be mine if you are here

I'm on the top of the world lookin' down on creation
And the only explanation I can find
Is the love that I've found, ever since you've been around
Your love's put me at the top of the world

I'm on the top of the world lookin' down on creation
And the only explanation I can find
Is the love that I've found, ever since you've been around
Your love's put me at the top of the world

Abraham / Jerry & Esther Hicks

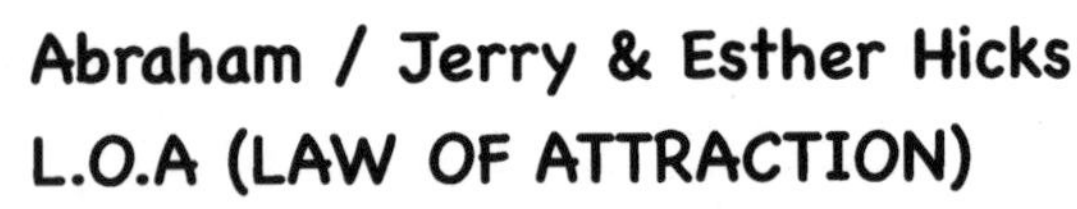

L.O.A (LAW OF ATTRACTION)

What you Focus on - you will always get more of ❣

So ask yourself - What are you really focusing on ...

that - which your emotions are ultimately attached to?

It is your emotions that signal to you, what the universe is matching & responding to.

So what energy frequency are you choosing to tune to?

Donna Eden & David Feinstein

They teach ENERGY MEDICINE.

Donnas daily energy routine is a great start to any day, for anyone going through anything - or, just wanting to focus on well-being ❣

Learn & adopt some of these simple tools ...

& everything else that follows - will simply just flow with new ease!

Wayne Dyer
MY FAVORITE QUOTE OF HIS IS
"When you change the way you look at things...
the things you look at change"

Mind Valley
by founder Vishen Lakhiani
There is Something for everyone at Mind Valley!
A Central place where you will find many talents ...
with personal stories you can relate to -
maybe - even find a mentor & learn something new!

Hay House & All of the wonderful mentors.
A go to place - where one feels at home ...
with so much wisdom to choose to indulge in.
Louise Hay
My Favorite Quote Of Hers Is
"I do not fix problems. I fix my thinking.
Then problems fix themselves.'

Stephen Black
A lovely British Clairvoyant
One Talented bloke, who tells it straight out - 'like it is'!
What Stephen reveals is amazing!
Doesn't always resonate immediately ...
but, with a lil patience & time -
the light bulb will be lit...
&, you will be amazed in the best way!

Joe Dispenza
My Favorite Quote Of His Is
"Behave, Believe, Become"
If you want the scientific explained with an interest in neuroscience etc.
The BRILLIANT Joe Dispenza is your go to guy.

Marisa Peer (another Brit)
I Graduated her online school &
became a Rapid Transformational Hypnotherapy Practitioner.
A great addition into my experiences.
Marissa teaches a multitude of therapies -
cleverly put together forming RTT.
Marisa focuses on the concept that we don't feel enough!
& the words that follow I AM follow you!

I learned this quote from Marisa
"The feeling that cannot find its expression in tears,
may cause other organs to weep"
by Dr. Maudsley

Jay Shetty
(Another Brit - Once a Monk)
I Enjoy his quotes & shares on Instagram - relatable!
Some interesting podcasts too ...
which, is just what the many enjoy - maybe, need!

Herman Siu
A 6th generation Shaolin Temple Descendant
He shares ancient wisdoms & so much more.
I had a call with Herman after some drastic life changes -
Amazing intuitive detail.
He does not disappoint!

Ho'
opono
pono

I'm Sorry!
Please Forgive Me!
Thank you!
I Love You!

A very simple Hawaiian prayer ...
when repeated 3X daily ...
seems to help one shed all that dead weight -
being carried on your shoulders.
The dead weight being treated like it is treasure!
The dead weight we don't need to be carrying with us.
It's the past!
It's called the past, because that is were it is meant to stay!
Just as the present is our gift of now!

Are You Choosing Now?
Your past can only be in your now - if you drag it here!

On a personal note - I have slowly become a frequent meditator.
I enjoy connecting to all in source energy only.
It brings about some interesting & loving feelings,
one can only describe as ...
intriguing, a joyful ease of knowing -
that our spirit energy never dies - to be so true!

The best intuitive meditation I ever had was outside in nature,
as I enjoyed being reclined in my **zero gravity recliner**.
If you have trouble relaxing into a meditation -
I would highly recommend the zero gravity recliner.
For those of us who like space in a chair -
the extra wide one is most comfortable for sure.

As I get ready to meditate -
I often set an intention of sorts.
Always positive of course!

I'd recommend starting out with some of the following:
Thank you - for allowing me to feel the love my higher power sees in me 

Thank you Source
(Father in the power of spirit, God, Jesus, Jehovah, Allah, Mohamed, Higher power, Dearly Divine - or however you choose to recognize)
Are we not all one Energy Source?

I appreciate the joy I get to experience in these meditation moments.

I am 'greatful' for healing breathing - I am so naturally capable of.
& of course...

Ho' opono pono

I'm Sorry
Please Forgive Me
Thank You
I Love You

This very simple easy read -
yet straight forward book, has been gathered
without sophisticated language intentionally.

To encourage any person - from ANY walk of life,
to see their WITHIN & AMAZING AUTHENTIC SELF WORTH!

My hope is... that **you choose** -
to reach beyond the ego, materialism, pre-paved patterns
& outside influences that have, & / or
do distract you - from your authentic self.
Life today with all the external influences...
many at our fingertips (literally!) -
the authentic self is easily sidelined, from being your priority.

I believe ...
the many questions presented to you in this forum -
will encourage you to look inwards,
as you lovingly choose to embrace yourself to date.
Your quest awaits you to knowing, growing & blooming
your authentic self - for your greatest good,
those around you & the world as a whole!

This book set up does not contain long winded chatter -
but rather, more of the shorter bursts -
that we are now accustomed to.

Keeping the content as short as possible became a priority -
since shorter attention spans are seemingly more & more familiar.

There is no need to be looking for answers to the many questions - if -
they do not fit your life to date.
But, could such subjects need addressing in your future... possibly?!
(or, helpful to someone you may know - possibly?).

Whatever be the case...
revisiting this book when appropriate - may be of help ...
with clarifying more thought & behavior patterns etc.

I believe - we all know ourselves best -
& have all the answers within us.
All that is required to live a better, fuller, happier, loving,
joyful life experience.
& this is why - you will find the many simple direct questions -
in this small self help book - of some service to you ❣
That being said, totally depends of course ...
if you choose to answer with complete honesty for yourself❣

I have found that - many cannot afford a life coach or hypnotherapy sessions.
Many are still nervous of hypnotherapy, believing they will lose control.
Others simply cannot delve into complete honesty...
with anyone outside of themselves!
They have a fear of judgement or of exposing truths & secrets etc.
& so - their progress cannot be as desired or for their greatest good.
One can only be helped on such avenues - when honesty is divulged...
allowing an open pathway to ones greatest good!

As my friend Anna often says...
"The worst truth - is better than the best lie"

& so...
Do you see ... ?
Only you can answer for you because ...
your experiences are unique to you & only you!
Your perception is what matters!

Ultimately, it is my hope for you -
that as you read through this book -
it will lead you to all kinds of mindful possibilities.
All the while learning to feel - the love & appreciation of yourself ❣
If you are reading this publication,
it is because ...
you have chosen to self navigate ...
a different route through your life at this time.
You will, at least, learn - to be aware of your choices in real time
& not as an after fact ❣
Catching ones thoughts when they do not serve you -
or your greatest good is key!
Because ...
when you change your thinking... you change your life ❣

As individuals, we can all read the same questions & statements,
but - have completely different answers & reactions.
This is due to our personal experience & expectations ...
whether realistic or not.

Truth is ... if you can think it - it is possible in the right conditions.
Conditions = Ask, Believe It Is, Tune to It, Relax & Receive!

The hope is, you will simply go through a process of feeling...
IMPOSSIBLE -> **I AM POSSIBLE !**
IMPERFECT -> **I AM PERFECT !**
UNWORTHY -> **I AM WORTHY !**

& knowing what is your birthright
DISCOVERING & CONNECTING WITH YOUR AMAZING AUTHENTIC SELF
For some it could be ...
the most worthwhile bumpy ride - you ever experienced!
& for others it may simply mean adjusting a little here & there -
rather easily.
Baby steps for some are big changes - true?
But - once momentum takes place - there are no limits in reaching

It all really depends on your viewpoint from your standpoint.
As your position changes so may your view point.

Can you be open minded enough - for your greatest good?

You may well find - you learn - how to easily shed -
what no longer serves you!
That you catch those unruly thoughts, actions & reactions
not only related to your past -
but your present - your now!
This in turn affects your future, that quickly becomes your now

That you ... Yes, you my busy friend - much like the amazing honey bee...
you have your very own vibration & frequency ...
that awaits your best connection!
So get ready to be **honest** with yourself &...
tune into your best you!
Be willing to align with your authentic self because you are worthy!

You will simply learn to understand - you can be perfectly you - in your life...
& proudly say - **'THIS IS MY LIFE!'**
Because, **'THIS IS MY CHOICE'** - as you acknowledge & accept
every action & reaction that follows your every choice.

You can choose a life without negative continued patterns & labels
previously adopted or given to you - that no longer serve you!

Many - if not most of us assumed these patterns &
labels, even beliefs - to be the best or only option ...
because such patterns & labels ...
were, are & have been available at our finger tips!
Most of which are handed down to us ...
becoming a part of our belief system to date!

'If good enough for them,
then good enough for me attitude!' ...
was encouraged & / or expected!
True?
Going forward it will be a knowing -
that everything - is a choice - your choice!
& so... you can choose to continue on the same path,
or decide you want to know more of your worth.

You can **choose** to change course because...
you desire more of what you deserve -
in this human life experience.

Remember ...
you are choosing the choice, action & chain reaction
attached to your every decision - even in avoiding an issue -
you my busy friend are making a choice!

At a young age - like most of you I'm sure ...
I truly did believe my parents knew everything!
I had great parents - who always did their best!
Most parents do, based on their individual capacity - true?
I did not realize, until I became an older adult myself -
that life is a rollercoaster of lessons we choose without realizing ...
realizing that we are doing the choosing!
Every choice, every action is a reaction & has a chain reaction regardless!

New ways of thinking may feel scary at first, due to being unfamiliar -
but my busy friend...
Life will take on greater meanings, in so many ways - as you -
(Re-) connect with your authentic energy vibing self.

Influences available at your finger tips with todays algorithms & funnels -
are mostly assumed to mean "popular" !
This is largely untrue because - it is not always positively popular -
if at all!

As my friend Leilani says
"The things that are right are not always popular
& the things that are popular are not always right."

Any online search will automatically send you like things or ...
the higher paying companies will be boosted ahead of others...
just like magic to the many minds!
But, it is actually -
a preprogrammed smart feature on your electronic of choice.

This reminds me of a cute story!
A great niece of mine wanted something - as kids do!
She asked her mother if she could have it.
Her mother told her "there's no money to buy it."
To which she responded...
"then just go to the hole in the wall for it then!"
(The hole in the wall being a term used for an ATM machine)
This lil story demonstrates how the young often - yet innocently
interpret what they see!
(money coming out of the machine in the wall when you want or need to go shopping)

So ask yourself - What do you see or
What have you seen & Interpret very differently to
what is, & / or was?

I challenge you to focus on "THE GREATEST GOOD OF ALL"
(Greater does not always mean Greatest!)
& So why not think **for the Greatest Good?**
Then simply watch the Universe magically -
yet lovingly conspire beyond funnels &
algorithms for ultimate amazement ❣
Magical Joy at its best!

YOU ARE WORTHY MY BUSY 🐝 FRIEND!
YOU TRULY NEED TO BELIEVE IN YOURSELF!

WHEN YOU BELIEVE -
THEN YOU CAN TUNE IN...RELAX & RECEIVE!

No matter your age, your gender, goal, habit or issue...
with your will to look at yourself to your core -
you have what it takes to pursue & live up to your
authentic full potential!

You are Imperfectly Perfect! Do you see that?
Why not change it to I am perfectly Perfect,
on this journey - to my Unique Authentic Self?

You have a journey of amazing possibilities -
awaiting your choosing!

As you read through this book -
you will find many subjects with the many questions -
only you can answer for you!

The layout leaves a lil extra room for your personal notes,
answers, thoughts, doodles etc.
There is never enough space in the margins of a general layout - IMO!

Intentionally, Some of the content on many pages
are specifically there to be thought inducing & / or thought provoking
on purpose - with purpose ❣

You will find some pictures - that represent love & nature etc.
in the hope to induce & / or provoke pleasant thought feelings ❣
The gems represent the gem that you are ❣

How amazing is the earth we live on -
that water ways can mimic beautiful tree shapes?
I witnessed wonderful views from a plane ride when leaving Gibraltar, showing how bodies of water branch off smaller & longer into other areas close by - such beauty

YOUR NEW YEAR STARTS NOW
YOUR NEW YOU
NEW CHOICES - NEW FEELINGS - NEW JOY

STARTS TODAY IF YOU SO CHOOSE!

N - New

E - Eternal

W - Ways

Y - You

E - Eagerly

A - Act

R - Repeatedly

WHAT OF THE FOLLOWING WORDS CAN YOU UNDERLINE - THAT EITHER...
DESCRIBE YOU OR WHAT YOU FEEL ABOUT YOURSELF?
CIRCLE THOSE YOU WISH TO BE

HAPPY / SAD
GOOD / BAD
TENSE / RELAXED
EVOLVED / EVOLVING
STRESSED / BLESSED
SCATTERED / FOCUSED
APPRECIATED / TAKEN FOR GRANTED
NEEDED / WANTED
NURTURED / NEGLECTED
BRAVE / SCARED
TENSE / CALM
STUCK / MOTIVATED
INSECURE / FEARLESS
RANDOM / INTENTIONAL
CONFIDENT / POWERLESS
HARMONIZED / CHAOTIC
BORING / SMART
TALENTED / GIFTED
TREASURED / VALUED
EASE & FLOW / STRUGGLE
LOVED / HATED
SIMPLE / COMPLICATED
INDEPENDANT / DEPENDANT
ILLNESS / WELLNESS
NEGATIVE / POSITIVE
LESS / MORE
OPEN / CLOSED
STRONG / WEAK
BUSY / RELAXED
IMBALANCED / BALANCED

DISCUSS / ARGUE
HEALTHY / UNHEALTHY
PROBLEM / SOLUTION
VITAMINS / PILLS
SKINNY / FAT
EAT TO TASTE / EAT TO MAINTAIN
WOUNDED / HEALED
USED / ABUSED
SPEAK YOUR TRUTH / DELUSIONAL
BROKEN / FIXED
PLEASURE / PAIN
LOVE / HEARTBREAK
DARKNESS / LIGHT
LIVE IT / ENJOY IT
RESTED / UNRESTED
POOR / OK / WEALTHY
DRIFTING / DOING
VALUED / GIFTED
LOVED / LOVABLE
TRUSTING / UNTRUSTING

IS YOUR GLASS HALF FULL OR GLASS HALF EMPTY?
ARE YOU THE PRIZE? OR YOU WANT THE PRIZE?
DOES IT MATTER HOW YOU DIE OR HOW YOU LIVE?

OUR LIFE IS MUCH LIKE
A RAIN DROP
AS IT EXPLODES INTO
A BEAUTIFUL CROWN OF WATER 

MAGNIFICENT IF YOU CHOOSE ❣

ALWAYS ON THE BRINK-ING EDGE

Get the feeling…

you are always
on the brink -

of something
great?

You sense it, feel it -

but can't quite touch it

Maybe you need help brainstorming…

to enjoy what joys your journey holds for you.

Or could you already know where your joy waits

&

you need assistance planning your path to it?

Oh the things to ponder on your Brink

I believe, no matter who we worship - & / or whether or not we follow an organized religion - it is the same source of energy...
from where our energy originated ❣️

S - SEARCHING

O - OBVIOUS

U - UNSOURCED

R - ROUTINE

C - COLLECTIVE

E - ENERGY

O - ONLY

N - NOW

E - ENERGY

WILLINGNESS!

The willingness to change for better habits is growth!

What are you willing to change & why?

Who are you willing to change for?

It should be you

What matters & filters down stream -

is what you matters to you

You can choose to be your best friend or
your worst enemy - true?

What matters to you most & why?

How willing are you - to matter to you?

Your willing, your able ...

just choose wisely ...

you deserve to be your best friend

YOUR VERY OWN HERO 

The oldest tree on the Island of Gibraltar

It has Amazing Life Growth!

Wouldn't your life represent the love & growth

if it was as mature as an old tree?

Everyone knows that being in nature &
experiencing natural beauty helps us...
mentally, emotionally & Beyond!

So imagine you are a tree!
Your roots ground you &
are your Energy Connection to ...
the beautiful earth we live on.
Your roots are labelled -
Thoughts, Beliefs, Vibrations & Frequency.

Each bark pattern is a pathway of choices you made
as you have navigated life to date!
These choices lead to action, reactions -
& ultimately consequences!
Consequences with both positive & negative results - true?
But, always teaching you something of value - true?
Did you recognize the value?

Each pathway brought you to an intersection, that broke off into a branch.
This branch forked off into 2 more branches of "choosings."
Each of these 2 branches then branched off into 5 more branches...
with 5 more choices in choosing!

Isn't this your life to date?
As you grew - did you learn well?
Reaching a point of further decision making...
as you chose which pathways to take!

When we are young - many choices are made for us...
influenced by our parents & guardians - true?
Sometimes through influencers -
& organized religions too!

Sometimes we change course - plan(t) a new tree
& still choose the same familiar pathways -
that lead us exactly to the same result - True?
Thus ending in an all too familiar place -
right where we started.
But is it where you wanted to be?

Sometimes the long pathway -
is the shortest route -
it blossoms beautifully into more
along the way!
Just the adventure & experiences we require
to fully bloom -
bloom into a person that feels quite well
within!

When you have reached the end of all 5 branches -
your decisions you made - can now be seen -
possibly even sparking great Joy, from joyful experiences along the way!

& just like life...
some leaves & branches will break off or die off - when their time is done!
Others will continue to blossom year in - year out -
reaping the benefits of the nutritional seeds
that have been sewn into their roots.

Now, wouldn't you like to design your own life path...
Using a new tree as a form of guidance -
that is rather simple to adopt?

C.S Lewis once said...
"You can't go back & change the beginning,
but you can start where you are
& change the ending."

And remember...
You can always plan(t) a new tree
to grow in this chapter of your life (your now)
& watch it take on new meaning...
Season to Season!

Plan(t) with intention, grow with each life season & choose your own path!

So just like the tree...

You have roots - that may or may not have grown deep.
These roots hold the millions of thoughts you have had to date.
(& will hold the many thoughts yet to come) ...
Many of these thoughts formed or are forever forming your belief system.

Your feelings & emotions run deep on many levels -
with the many subjects, from your life experiences - true?

These feelings & emotions give off vibrations...
that form frequencies that the universe responds to...
every moment of every waking day .

As you grow & learn in this human experience we call life...
you have free will to choose on many levels - true?

Many of your choices are influenced, guided, possibly demanded - true?
Much like the tree being influenced by the weather &...
it's nutrients from intake at the root level.

For the tree as the seasons change, the weather changes & ...
the trees growing slows - even changes / or ...
depending where in the world it resides, may become dormant - true?
Are we not the same to a large degree?

For some - their growth pattern is stunted from the lack of nutrition!
For others, their pathways are influenced by their elders, care givers etc.
All of these choices & influences involve feelings & emotions -
ultimately giving off a vibration & frequency!

The Universe responds to our feelings & emotions -
as this is our true present living feeling vibration & frequency!

The tree trunk can be compared -
to the pathways of our years as they add up -
whether we choose to take such pathways, or ...
we are influenced - maybe even pushed towards them - true?

The older we get (hopefully wiser) -
we learn that free will ... is the choice!
To use that free will for our greatest good! BUT, ARE YOU?

As we branch out into the world & hopefully bloom repeatedly ...
we are constantly looking to enhance our blooming - correct?
Are we not always looking for the help needed?
Which brings me to the most important question of all!
THE TITLE OF THIS BOOK!

Where Is The Help I Need? (1st letter of each word is your answer)

```
 |     |  |   |    | |
 \     \  \   \    \ \
  \     |  |   |    | |
   W    I  T   H    I N
```

THAT'S RIGHT!
THE ANSWER IS **WITH** YOU!
THE ANSWER IS **IN** YOU! **WITHIN !**

W - WHEN

I - I

T - THINK

H - HERE

I - IN

N - NEUTRAL

When you get to the this -
you are no longer in judgement ❣

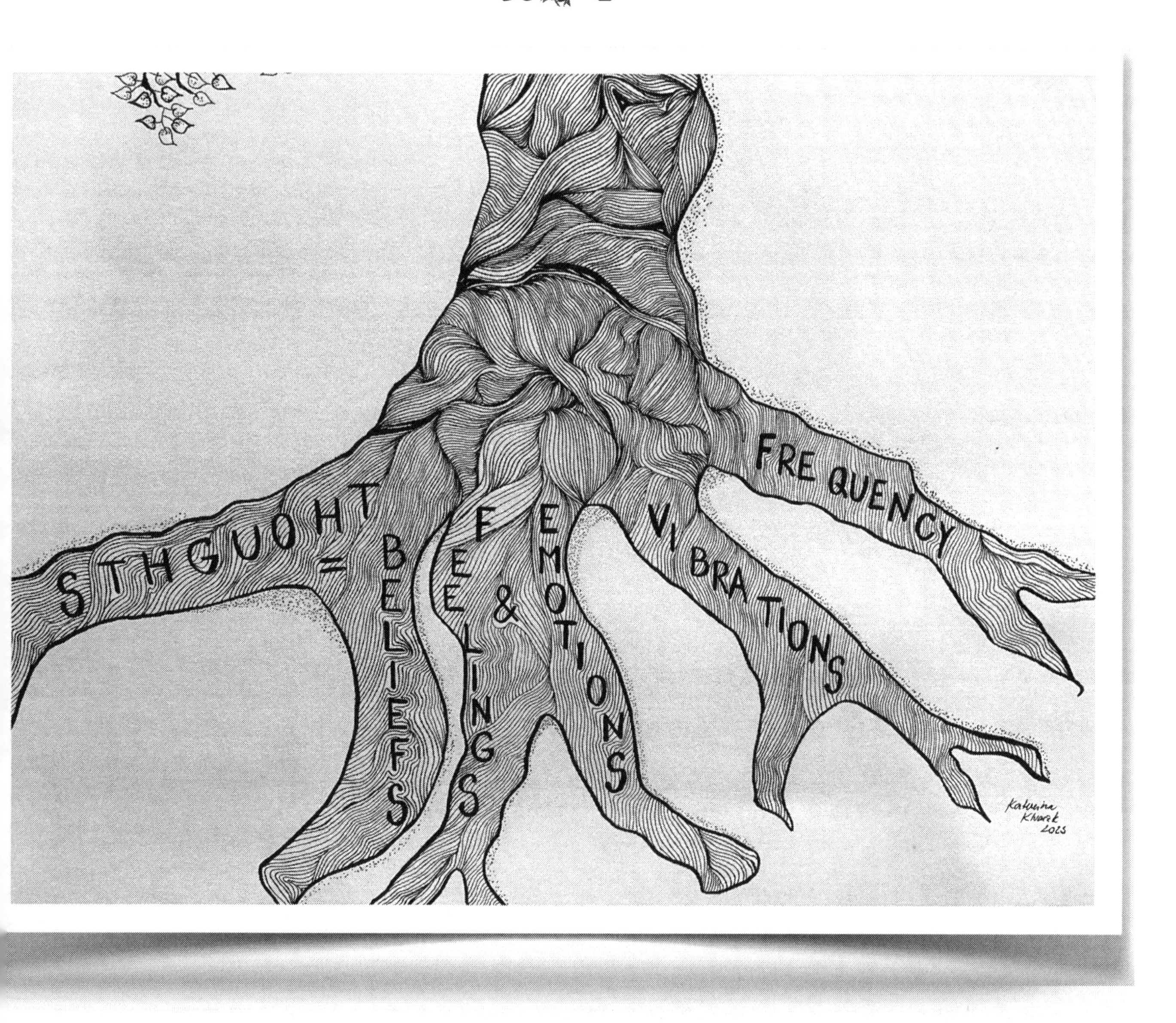

If our thoughts are often quite backwards -
then what may our beliefs be?
Our feelings & emotions are valid, as is our guidance - true?
Then what vibrations & frequency do we have as a result?

Our thoughts are many...
up to 60-70,000 thoughts per day.
& mostly repeated day in / day out -
without giving this pattern a 2nd thought!

Would you agree our thoughts are often backwards - maybe negative?

Would you also agree - we can be accepting of thoughts that -
don't feel right because...
we maybe, care more about how the external influences see us -
or accept us ...
more - than we care to listen to our internal true guidance?

You know that internal little voice ...
the one that whispers every so often to you!
It is there to help navigate your human experience - known as life!

Your beliefs are yours - true?
Where & how did they develop?

Are your feelings & emotions in conflict -
with the beliefs you are so dearly holding onto?
Then, what kind of vibrations & frequencies are you?
- or + ?

WHERE DID YOUR BRANCHES GROW FROM?

YOUR ROOTS CAME 1ST - CORRECT?

THEN CAME YOUR PATHWAYS - TRUE?

THEN YOU BRANCHED OUT HERE & THERE -
THEN A FEW MORE TIMES - ALL TRUE - YES?

INSIDE YOU GREW TOO - TRUE?

IS IT AS PRETTY ON THE INSIDE AS IT IS ON THE OUTSIDE?

IF YOUR MANY THOUGHTS ARE ANYTHING TO DECIDE BY ...
WHAT WOULD YOU CONCLUDE?

YOUR TRUE WONDER LIES **WITH-IN** YOU!

THE QUESTION YOU MUST DECIDE IS...
DO YOU WANT TO SEE & BE - WHO YOU ARE AUTHENTICALLY?

IF YOU CHOOSE TO PLANT YOUR OWN SEEDS,
FEED & GROW THOSE ROOTS -
WHAT WONDER - WOULD YOU EXPECT TO SEE OR WANT TO SEE?

CAN YOU ACKNOWLEDGE YOU - YES YOU -
HOLD THE ANSWERS YOU SEEK **WITH-IN?**

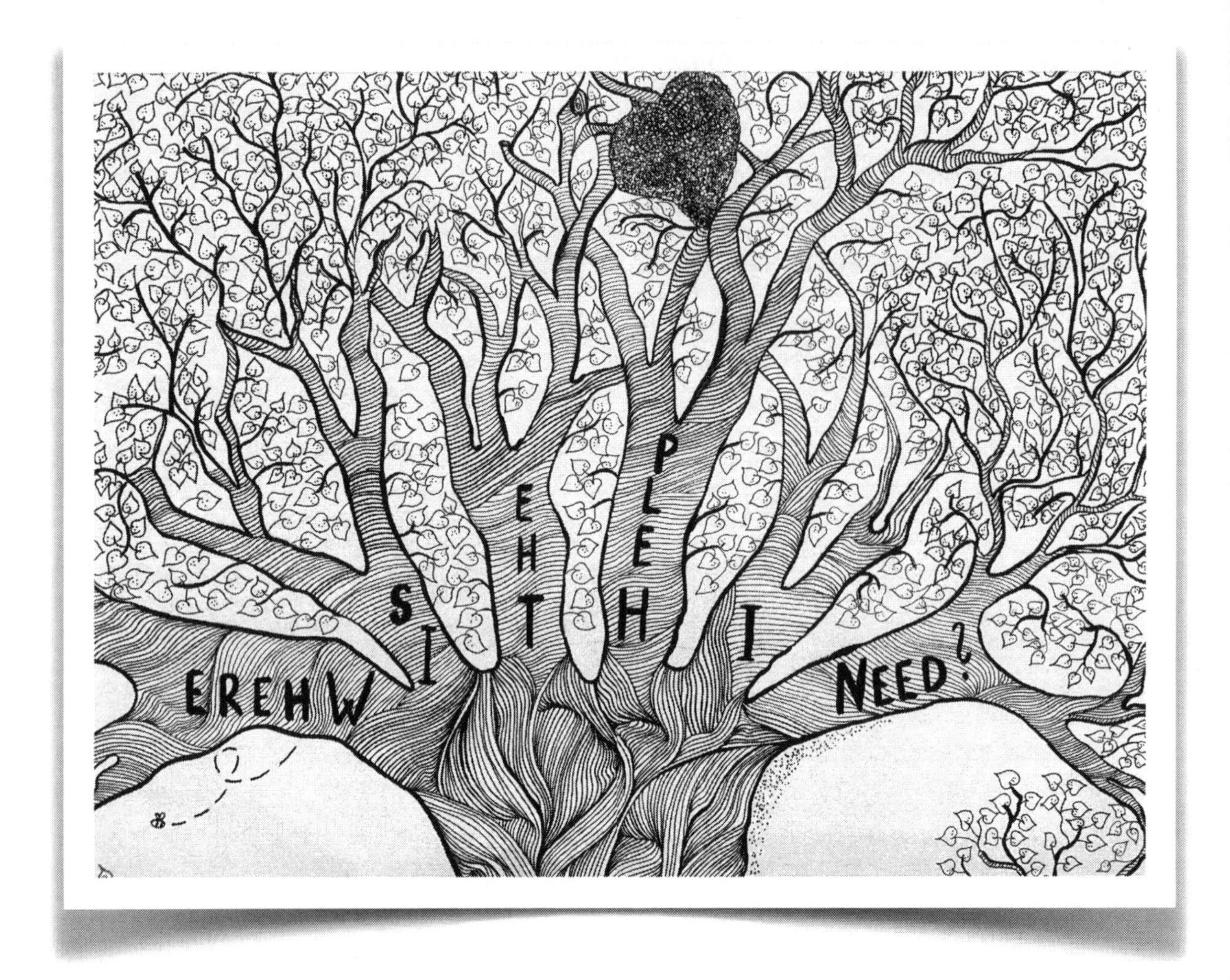

Where - my busy friend are you looking for help?

Do you actually need the help you seek?

Could it be your looking anywhere & everywhere outside of yourself?

Isn't it time you looked with-in?

EVALUATE YOURSELF

Have you ever evaluated yourself - with the goal to align?
The same way you would evaluate another human -
to be suitable of you, your time, your attention & your love?

This can be a good start to evaluating
your body - your mind - your beliefs!

How does your body feel?
Do you know or know why?

Out of habit?
Lack of nutrition?
Lack of general love & self care?

How does your mind feel?
Do you know or know why?

From Habit of thought?
Lack of positive influences?
Lack of overall consideration about how you truly feel?

Who Are You Vibing With?

Who is in your vibe tribe?

Do you know?

Do you even know - your own vibe?

Are they family, friends, strangers, colleagues, etc.?

Is it mostly good, all good, less than mostly good, or -

not even close to good?

Do you know why?

You can choose who you vibe with - based off -

what you vibe at ❣

Do you even stop & think about yours, or -

your tribes vibe ?

You are free to choose your vibe tribe - True?

What vibe are you Choosing? Using? Abusing? & Why?

How Valuable Are You?

What is your personal value?

Have you ever even thought about it?

You are priceless my busy friend

If you believe someone has the right to tell you your worth ...

Or

believed what someone told you your worth is....

then you are truly somewhere in the unworthy zone sadly :-(

A zone you were given, born into & / or experienced - true?

It is your birthright to **believe in yourself** 

Not easy or remotely familiar to the many - it's so sad :-(

Because, it is your birthright - to be worthy of all your desires
- for your greatest good

Belief in your greatest good of self -
is the greatest gift you can give yourself

Forgive yourself for not grasping this reality sooner 

Go on - look in that mirror & say **'I FORGIVE YOU!'**

Your journey of **worthiness** can begin a new,
with every new day❣

You can choose how worthy you are, then choose to align.
Then believe it (you must feel worthy of it) -
so you can receive it❣

Worthiness awaits your undivided attention -
Acknowledge your you❣

When you believe it - the good in the world believe it too❣

If you had a plant - you would feed & water it - true?
So what are you feeding & watering yourself with -
my busy 🐝 friend?
Today you can choose to feed & water yourself your worth 

You are
priceless
my busy 🐝
friend❣

Ride Your Rocket of What You Want!

Want to ride your rocket of what you truly want?

Choose a better feeling thought!

Want to ride the rocket of creation?

Choose to do your own creating!

Want to ride the wave of a better -

day, week, month, year, life?

Tell yourself the better -

but same story until you can

almost hear it, feel it, see it,

taste it, touch it!

Be ready to ride your rocket!

Get Ready to be ready -

for your rocket awaits you -

to believe, relax & receive!

A **belief** is a thought most often handed down to you
from family, school, church, influencers etc. -
truly thoughts you give attention to & **keep thinking**!

So are your thoughts out of habit?
Lack of learning to know **you** can choose to think -
your own individual thoughts on many levels?

Do you have a lack of belief in yourself -
when same or similar like minded people
are not in your daily experience?

Are you sacrificing yourself -
Your true inner you?
As you conform & fit in -
with those around you?

Do you feel you have a purpose bigger than -
your daily, weekly, monthly, yearly life?

Do you even know who you are at your core?
The you without the many influences that surround you?

Do you want to know your purpose -
for your human experience?

Be still!

Be silent!

Be patient with yourself!

Listen to your heart, your mind, your body - your inner you!

Your **inner you** really does know
how marvelous you truly are!

Because - your inner part of you believes in you!

Believes in the greatest good of you!
It is time you Listened & Let That Be **Your Greatest Influence** ❣

If something feels wrong - then it is wrong for you!

But - be sure to know…

there is a difference between feeling wrong, versus an unfamiliar feeling!

So ask yourself - could this just be unfamiliar?

Find your inner you - that inner good feeling

& know what feels right for you!

Then get focused in that feeling -

that knowing -

you are in charge of You

& Your Choices ❣

Align with your you❣

Your - I Love You ❣

YOUR WITHIN IS ...

Y - YOU
O - OWN
U - UNLIMITED
R - RESOURCES

WITH YOU - IN YOU !

YOU ARE YOUR OWN HERO !

H - HEARTFELT
E - EXPERIENCES
R - REMAIN
O - ONGOING

WITHIN !

Healthy Limit(s) & Boundaries = Love of Self & Those Around You
(Often your nearest & Dearest)

What do your personal limit(s) & boundaries (your operating manual) consist of?
You can write your own operating manual as you read through this book answering the many questions - with the greatest good of self & others in mind.
Change & challenge yourself to write a list of 7 limits & boundaries ... that you have now & again at the end of this book.
It would also be wise of you - if you can describe from an emotional standpoint - when you think of these limits & boundaries.

1/
My emotions around this are....

2/
My emotions around this are....

3/
My emotions around this are....

4/
My emotions around this are....

5/
My emotions around this are....

6/
My emotions around this are....

7/
My emotions around this are....

WHAT ARE YOUR LIMITS?

What are your limits & boundaries ?

Are they equal to the love of self & those around you?

OR

Are these boundaries in disguise like a small cage -

that you imprison yourself in - out of fear?

Your thoughts & feelings can be of the negative past -

that you keep bringing to your present - true?

You **can** simply choose to find a better feeling thought

repetitively - until it becomes the 'new norm'!

THE NEW BETTER FEELING - THE FREER FEELING YOU

Again I ask what limits & boundaries are you choosing?

4 C's of Limits
Can / Cannot / Choose / Correct

Who limits who?

Truth is…….

You limit you ❣️

Whether you believe you **can** …

Or You believe you **cannot**…

You will always be **correct** ❣️❣️❣️

For what you Repeatedly Tell Yourself

Will become your Belief ❣️

Read that again ❣️❣️❣️

So ask yourself - How Do You Limit You?

Choose LIMITLESS ❣️

Choose LIMITLESS YOU ❣️❣️❣️

The diversity in nature with its trees are amazing!

There is no discrimination❣️

There is only growth, bloom, shed & rest!

A pattern that is worth following - true?

Quite possibly ❣️

E - ETERNAL

N - NEVER

E - ENDING

R - RADIANT

G - GRAVITATIONAL

Y - YOU

FOCUS

What is your focus today?

Is it worthy of your attention?

Where your attention goes...... energy flows 

Do you know where your energy is going?

Are you choosing to put your attention ...

& your energy where it best serves you?

If you can only focus 100% on one thing at a time...

what, are you choosing to spend your time on?

FOCUS & FIND WHAT TRULY SERVES YOU...

BECAUSE YOU ARE WORTHY OF FINDING YOUR FOCUS 

Read that again !!!

What kind of **ENERGY** would best serve you? Do you even know?
So... if everything is energy - YES EVERYTHING!!!!!!!
Then everything vibrates at some form of frequency - TRUE?

The higher you raise your frequency - or
possibly best said as 'the more positive your frequency' -
the better you personally experience whatever it is you focus on!
(remembering of course that of which your emotions
are strongest about & / Or connected to).

The better **connected** you are **to** your inner you - **your authentic self**
along with **that heartwarming pleasing feeling in your heart** ...
that which allows you to easily find **appreciation in** ...
& / or of your **experiences**, then - **the better your frequency**.

When someone is upset about something & their frequency is dominant...
you will quickly see others in the vicinity start to vibrate (engage)
at that level -
even if only to be upset at the person dominating that frequency.
Kids (sadly) suddenly will get a belly ache or a sudden feeling of un-wellness!
(familiar?)

A telephone call, text message, movie, music,
are just to name a few - that can affect your vibration.
This is where choosing wisely benefits you.

If you can see it, hear it, smell it, taste it, touch it
or
imagine any of these - your vibration is affected by it.
And so I ask you...
what kind of energy will you allow to dominate your well being?

What will you choose to see, to hear, to smell, to taste & to touch
in your imagination & in your reality - for your greatest good?

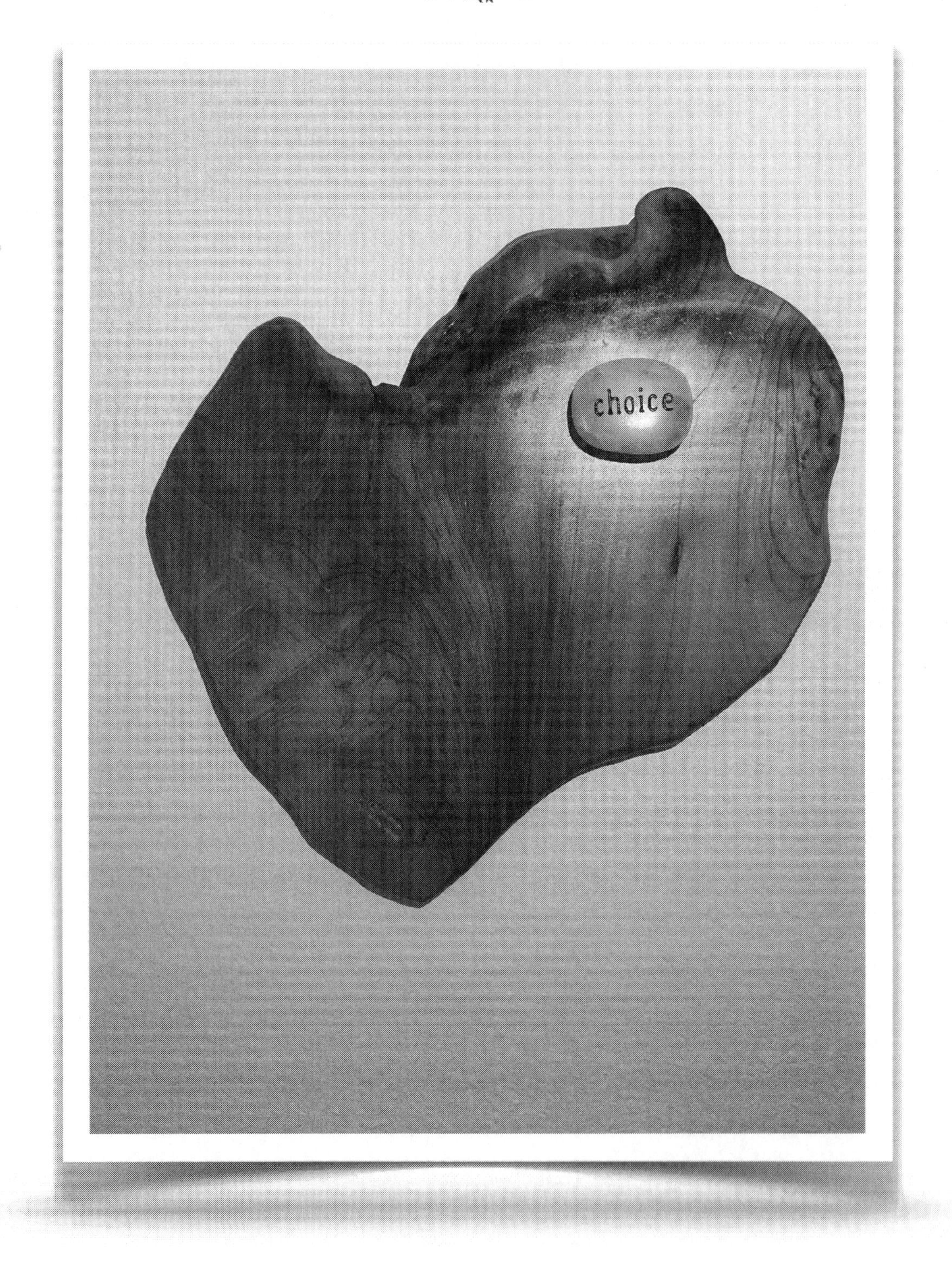

YOU HAVE THE FREEDOM TO CHOOSE!

ARE YOU CHOOSING WISELY?

Do you know that everything in life involves CHOICES?

Yes everything in your life Involves **your** choices!!!
Remember - we have **free will** to choose!

It is said that - we choose to come for the human experience -
even choosing our parents, knowing ...
that negativity will be a part of that experience.

Ask yourself ...
Are you making choices based on your authentic self?
or
Do your decisions depend on your many influences & adopted patterns?

<u>How Accountable Are You based On The Choices You Are Choosing?</u>

Do you consistently make the same choices ...
while expecting a different result?

Everything Involves Your Choices.
You can choose how to be, act, react etc!
True?

What's your choice?

What are you choosing between & why?

Is there a Rhyme & Reason to your choices?

I hope for you it is a choice - to be better & do better!

Is today your day for better choices?

This in itself is a choice because everything requires a CHOICE ❣️

CHOICE

C - Careful of your choices ❣

H - Happiness should be the goal result of your choices ❣

O - Open heartedly are the best choices ❣

I - Instant good feelings are the go to choices ❣

C - Create better choices ❣

E - Ecstatically making choices ❣

IT TAKES STRENGTH TO CHOOSE TO GROW ❣

Enjoy Choosing Your Thoughts!

Choose better feeling thoughts....

It might just change your life❣

Choose a good feeling thought....

It might just change your mood❣

Choose a happy thought......

It might just make you smile❣

Be better❣

Feel better❣

Smile more❣

Do it more & more & more 

THOUGHT SIFTING

Thought sifting some would say.....

Really depends on your end goal

or should one say -

a moving target.

If you sift well ...

your target will shift closer ...

even evolve into something bigger ...

maybe - even change!

Are you coming from a place of -

Love, Want, Need, or Necessary?

GET SIFTING

&

SHIFTING

De L

Are you Overthinking?

Thinking & Analyzing …….

Anything & Everything!

And for what?!

REALLY! For What? & Why?

Did you find Resolve?

All that time …..

All that energy gone …..

& Suddenly you realize how much time you have spent
stuck in THE MENTAL PRISON you put yourself in …..

Are you going nowhere fast - except for hopping on - the rollercoaster of stress & anxiety of what ifs!!!!!?

STOP! - TAKE A MOMENT! - WHAT IS YOUR TIME REALLY WORTH?

WHAT IS YOUR TIME VALUE?

WHAT IS YOUR ENERGY VALUE?

GIVE BETTER VALUE TO YOUR THOUGHTS!

KEEP IT SIMPLE!

Catch yourself & refocus!

BECAUSE - YOU ARE WORTH IT 

BELIEFS

What are your beliefs?

Are they yours or handed to you through family, friends,

church & the likes?

What beliefs would you prefer?

And why?

Can you make only good beliefs yours for the greater good?

OF COURSE YOU CAN❣

SIFT & SORT - KEEPING ONLY WHAT IS REALLY TRUE TO YOU❣

MAKE YOUR BELIEFS TRUE FOR YOU❣

YOU OWE IT TO YOU - YOU REALLY, REALLY, REALLY DO❣

Repeated Thoughts, Patterns & Labels = **BELIEFS**

What repeated thoughts, patterns & labels do you have?
A pattern can be a thought you keep thinking -
which then evolves into a **BELIEF!**
A pattern can be a reaction to something you experienced -
that you adopted - because you saw that same reaction daily
becoming a familiar pattern -
all the while forgetting that you have a choice.

eg: you were born without a fear of heat.....
you soon figured out either by guidance or
by actual touch - that heat can be dangerous!
So you develop - a pattern of action or
reaction in regards to heat.

eg: As a young child you may well have witnessed someone
go through fear or anxiety in a situation or experience!
You then adopted this as your coping mechanism
towards same & similar situations.
Almost an expected way of dealing with things ...
but - is it the real you or what you learned to do?

A Label may well be what someone called you repeatedly -
that became your belief & subconsciously you live up to that label.

eg: You were told you were lazy or stupid growing up &
now your older... when you think about doing something specific -
you talk yourself out of that specific something.
Are you telling yourself you are not smart enough or
do you not believe you have what it takes?
Have you adopted the why bother attitude reaction or lack of action?

ONLY YOU KNOW WHAT IS TRUE?

If you say it to yourself - (negative or positive) it will be true!

Is that lil voice in your head echoeing someone else's opinion?
Are you hearing - 'who do you think you are?'
If others are talking (positively or negatively) about you ...
as you reach or work for more -
the fact you are their actual topic of conversation means -
you should know your doing something right for you!
You should know & understand that their opinion is of zero consequence!
what matters is what you think & say to yourself!

If you tell yourself your smart &
believe you have what it takes to achieve...
it will be true!
You have that whispered to you every so often don't you?
Listen to those whispers
with that trail showing you sparks of joyful possibilities...
that joy - those possibilities are just for you my busy friend.

You know the difference between that lil voice &
that whisper don't you?
That lil voice is critical, doubting & crushes your spirit - true?
But that soft whisper that is gentle, lighter & much kinder ...
if you pay attention to that whisper -
for just a small fraction of time...
it is just the dose of encouragement required -
for you to take that step onto that pathway made just for you!

SO ASK YOURSELF - WHAT DO YOU WANT TO BE TRUE FOR YOU?
& What do you prefer to listen to - the voice or the whisper?

The heart can get pretty scarred & beaten up
in this human experience we call 'life' - true?

Is it not also true, as you receive the love & attention required
- you get back on your journey of positivity ...

& then the scars & holes start to fill in & beautifully so ❣

Give your heart the love & attention it deserves!

WANT, NEED, NECESSARY?

What do you really want?

Why do you really want it?

For the means to what end?

What do you really need?

Why do you really need it?

For the means to what end?

What is really necessary?

Why is it necessary?

For the means to what end?

Define, Refine, Reboot

& Achieve your Wants.... Needs..... & Necessaries....

for all the inner knowing right reasons

WITH INTENTION ❣

WITH CONTENTMENT ❣

WITH JOY❣

What's your **issue?**

Is it your issue or really someone else's issue that you have chosen to take on?

Does this issue consume your time ...
whether it be a minute, hour(s), day(s), week(s), month(s) or even years?

If any emotional issue is negatively repetitive...
it is for you to decide which tissue it ends in!

They say a problem shared is a problem halved!
Could this be true for you & your "said" issue...
while dumping out the emotions attached?

Is dumping these emotions into a box of tissues the preferred method?
or - do you run the risk of it festering into your body tissues...
possibly presenting as a disease someday?!

If it's a simple issue of what someone says or does in your presence...
but does not harm you or anyone else - then it is your issue - not theirs!
You need not react to an opinion outside of yourself - true?

If your are offended because someone was to identify differently to you - or
- to what is most familiar to you (knowing the brain likes familiar & dislikes
unfamiliar) - then this is your issue - not theirs.
Because it affects them - not you - true?

We are all energy & vibrate at our very own frequency ...
those with different preferences to what is seen as most familiar -
is only uncomfortable to those that vibrate at a different frequency, believing
their frequency be superior - since their familiar is seen as "the standard!"
The only true superior frequency is that of your original Source Energy
Creator! READ THAT AGAIN!!!
Should we not be wishing all the human race well on their journey -
for it may be a difficult path in discovering their best life ?

WHAT'S YOUR PATTERN?

Do you know your pattern of thought?

Is it positive or negative?

Do you know your pattern of action or reaction?

Is it for your greater good?

Do you even know if you are proactive or only reactive?

Something worthy of a ponder - no?

Is it serving you?

& if so - how?

Do you know if you are your own best friend or your worst enemy?

A hard question worth exploring - true?

All these mostly automatic patterns are familiar ...

But are they what's best for you?

So what is best for you?

Do you know?

Positive thought patterns lead to positive results -
Would you agree?

Can you catch each & every thought, action, reaction -
that does not serve you?

Then make that conscious choice for a better feeling thought... ?

A better feeling action, with a better feeling reaction...
That you are worthy of?

Do you even know you are worthy of better?

It is a choice to be your own best friend -
& do right by you in your thoughts, actions & reactions - true?

You are worthy of doing right by you...
Regardless of what influences surround you...

Because you have the CHOICE to let in -

that which influences you to your core ❣

READ THAT AGAIN ❣

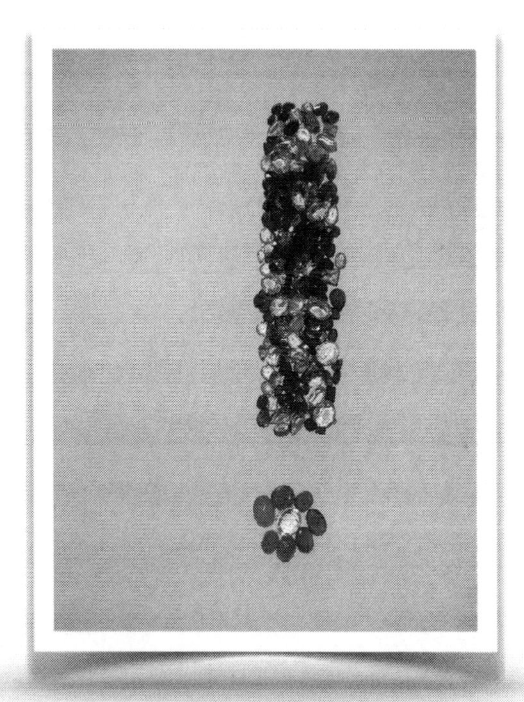

WHAT NO LONGER SERVES YOU?

Do you serve you?

What serving do those around you do?

Serve you & themselves too?

What does serve you?

What others can do for you?

Or

What you can do for others?

Do you hold onto what no longer serves you?

Do you?

Choose to do What serves you
with intention ...

Your purpose is a choice
to be well chosen ...

Because it feels right -

No?!

**AS we go through life &
discover our limits & boundaries ...
does your circle of trust get smaller
while your heart grows bigger?**

WHAT'S YOUR WORTH?

Do you think you are worth it?

Yes - You Should!

Are you worth that positive thought?

Yes - You Are!

Are you worth the time?

Damn Right You Are!

GIVE YOURSELF THAT TIME - YOU DESERVE IT! 

READ THAT AGAIN!

& AGAIN

& AGAIN!

Forgiveness Is A Necessity!

Can you forgive yourself ...

for not doing right by yourself?

You Really Should!

Can you forgive yourself ...

for not doing right by someone else?

You Really Should!

Can you forgive yourself ...

for time wasting of self, others &

whatever else passed / passes through your life's experience...

that which - stalled you getting to know you?

You Really Should!

LET IT GO ALREADY!

ENTER THIS NEW SEASON OF
YOU FREEING YOURSELF 💕

BECAUSE...

FORGIVENESS IS A NECESSITY !

HO' OPONO PONO

TO FREE YOURSELF &
TO PUT TO RIGHTS!

TO CORRECT, REVISE, TIDY-UP, ARRANGE, MANAGE & REGULATE!

I'M SORRY

Sorry is not only the word - but an action that backs up the word!

PLEASE FORGIVE ME 

Forgive yourself for your wrongs when others cannot & do not!

THANK YOU 

Be thankful of all your experiences - they brought you here!

I LOVE YOU 

Love because it is good for you & those around you!

REPEATING THESE 4 PRAYER STATEMENTS IN THE MIRROR TO YOURSELF
WILL ACTUALLY LIGHTEN YOUR LOAD
IN WAYS YOU CAN ONLY IMAGINE UNTIL YOU EXPERIENCE IT

Say it form the heart - you deserve it 

Be Your Own **Diva or Divo!**

What are your wants, needs & necessities Diva / Divo?

Do your Diva / Divo antics consist of anything beyond -
the dramatics of what you are trying to control?
What are you settling for?
Do you even know?

Why settle for anything less than what joy can bring
to your life experience?

So……What or Where can you get true joy from?
Do you know what Joy feels like?

Many forget that this is what the human experience is all about…
to find the **joy & love within** - **vibrating** at a level others see &
want some of -
I'm pretty sure many of you have heard …
" I'll have a pint, pound or gallon of whatever he or she is on"
at some point.

Joy is what you feel internally when …
you experience a true sense of happiness!
Happiness can be achieved on many levels - true?
In part by external influences - that bring your vibration up-leveling
to a higher positive feeling than previously experienced
to the event or action that sparked your Joy.

& so I ask you now -
do you want to make **choices** that…
can lead you to your authentic self - sparking those positive feelings…
of joy, of love & happiness dear Diva / Divo?

What Kind Of Selfish Are You?

The good at it kind - regardless of the negative input of others?

Because you know or learned, you are in charge of your life path experiences.

Quite Possibly!

**The kind that pleases themself no matter who it hurts, or ...
who it could affect in the process?**

**Because deep down - you feel undeserving, as you sabotage yourself & alienate you yourself - as you force this pleasing of self -
that can only hurt you the most - long term!**

Quite Possibly!

The kind that forgot self... unable to follow your hearts desire?

Because you put everyone before self (selfless = you give less to self)

& so not able to experience self joy!

Quite Possibly!

**Be the good kind - to be the change -
because you can!**

You Quite Possibly Can Be -

The Right Kind Of Selfish 💕

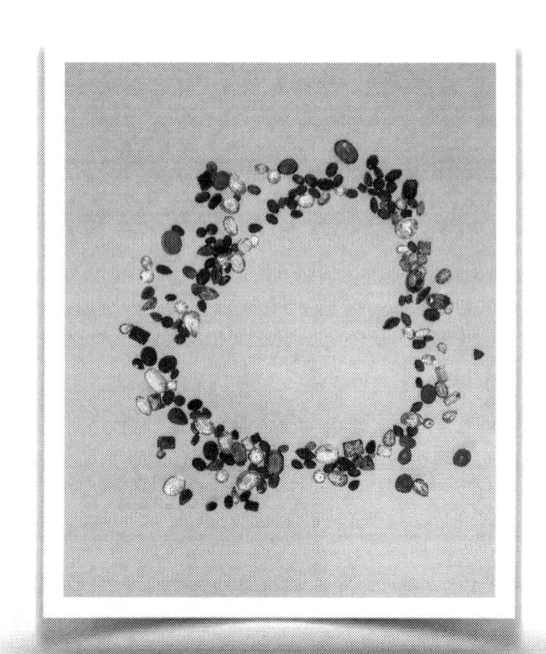

Words have power - would you agree?

We use them to communicate in this life we live - true?
So, what words are you choosing in your daily life?

Name those that are consistent in your life ...
& notice if they are positive or negative.

Are they mostly Negative, of complaining &
always in the lack of something?
If it is this way in general -
then what words are you repeating to yourself & others?

If you tell someone enough that they are this, that or the other -
it will eventually be believed.
Once believed, it can be received,
regardless if it's negative or positive influence.

Yes - Whatever it is you believe - will be true!

So why the over focus on the negative?

Turns out the mind focuses 2 1/2 times more on the negative...
because, its job is to keep you in survival mode.
In just knowing this particular fact -
it gives a lot more understanding to some of your responses in life - correct?

Challenge yourself to write those words that are negative in nature
& look to replace them with a positive.

For example - how many times have you said...
I'm starving! **INSTEAD OF** I'm experiencing hunger right now!
I'm dying! **INSTEAD OF** I'm experiencing a form of feeling exhausted!
I'm stressed! **INSTEAD OF** I'm experiencing a challenge!

Is it not easier on your mind & body to tell yourself -
you are experiencing something that is more true
over the original statement?

Write your own I am statements &
do the same changing of your statements to - I am experiencing ...

FEEL HOW THEY MAKE YOU FEEL!
NOTICE HOW YOUR MIND & BODY RESPONDS ...
AS YOU REPEAT THEM

I AM...

I AM EXPERIENCING...

I DO...

I EXPERIENCE...

OVERUSE OF BUT, WISH, HOPE & TRY

To say I'LL TRY is to ...

Accept you could fail!

To say I HOPE it works out ...

Leaves room for failure!

To say I WISH IT WAS ME about something ...

is believing it could only be available to someone other than you!

To add - BUT this or BUT that -

is allowing you to excuse yourself from achieving ... what you are desiring!

FEAR CAN CRIPPLE US INTERNALLY - TRUE?

DON'T FOCUS ON THE FEAR - as it will EXPAND!

FOCUS ON THE EXCITEMENT OF ACHIEVING A FORM OF JOY!!!

Amazing Fun Fact!

Did you know the brain has the same chemical reaction
regardless of it experiencing fear or excitement?

WISHING - wishing on a star they say -
is hope & inspiration - for the new horizon as it nears ❣

WISHING when blowing out your candles they say is ...
sending hope to the universe because ...
you have faith in the possibilities ❣

If there are any wishes worth exploring in your past -
it would be those ... that you did not get to experience.

Very likely - at no fault of your own, but more about
the inability of your caregiver I am sure ❣

What are all the things you wish you had heard as a kid?
We all have them - some of us not so many & some of us a lot.
But - you know the ones I am talking about - true?

We all stood & waited to hear something we knew we were - true?
But you never got that dose of clarification ...
that smile, that verbal pat on the back, etc!
Deflated, sad & possibly emotional on some level, where what was felt - true?

All you wanted & needed clarification on is that
you were...
beautiful, wonderful, brilliant, smart, amazing &
loved -
& that's just to name a few ❣

So write them all down but in present tense -
it is your present to yourself!
Tell that younger you everything he / she needed
to hear - in your now - read it back repeatedly
& follow that rainbow❣

For Example:

I am so thoughtful & kind because I care to share my me with you ❣

I am so kind & caring - always thinking of others too ❣

I am so creative - I create such wonderful, warm experiences ❣

1)

2)

3)

4)

5)

6)

7)

What clarification can you give to someone else ...
that deserves to hear how beautiful, wonderful, brilliant, smart, amazing
& loved they truly are?

What & Who are you **JUDGING** & why?

What is your message in this judging?
Jealousy?
Resentment?
Sadness of self?

Do you even realize you are delivering negative messages ...
to yourself in your judging attitude?

IF YOU ARE JUDGING OTHERS THEN YOU ARE LIKELY DOUBLING DOWN ON THE JUDGING OF YOURSELF WITHIN YOUR MANY THOUGHTS!

And So - in your opinion what are you?
Are you Shallow?
Lonely?
Unethical?
Dishonest With Others & Ultimately Yourself?
Yes Yourself!

For if you are behaving in any way towards others ...
then you are also doing this to yourself.
& this is why there is need to pause, when we are feeling uneasy about something. (off kilter so to speak)
For it is very likely this does not align - with your authentic self.

Are you often (or) capable of being any of the following - even temporarily?
Bratty / Bitchy / Materialistic / Mean / Demanding / Aggressive / Competitive / Conniving / Energy Sucking?
You are doing this to your self too!

Any of the afore mentioned states are equal to ...
you not being your true authentic beautiful, wonderful,
amazing self?

What does being any of the previously stated negative traits ...
tell you about you?
Are you liking what you see?

Can you be a better version of yourself in your here & now?
(of course you can!)

We all judge so easily when it is not familiar to us - but is it right?

Your inner you... so wants you to be real & authentic...
Because it induces a BLISS feeling of self ❣

A Love of self ❣

When you can love yourself authentically...
you have the ability to give unconditional love...
& in turn receive unconditional love too ❣

What would the better version of you feel like?
Describe this version of you in detail ❣

When you come from a place of love...
the world as you know it - is brighter, lighter & satisfying ❣

Do you think if you are judging - you are satisfied?

READ THAT AGAIN ❣

WILLINGNESS

The willingness to change to better habits is growth!

What are you willing to change & why?

Who are you willing to change for?

It should be you

What matters and filters down stream...

is what you matter to you

You can choose to be your best friend

or your worst enemy - true?

What matters to you most & why?

How willing are you to matter to you?

Your are willing & you are able?

Able to choose wisely - TRUE?!

You deserve to be your own best friend -

So Stop Judging You &

Negatively Opinon-ing On What's In & Outside of Yourself

What do you spend your time trying to **control** externally & why?

When your focus is on the external -
while attempting to control all kinds of variables……
You are really telling the universe you are (feeling)
out of control on the inside.

Your inner you, your self chatter, your self thoughts,
are not to your advantage in this state of control.

Do You Truly Think You Can Feel Better ...
Controlling What Is Around You?
Instead Of having some form of Understanding &
actually deciding to Choose - to just let it be or let it go & trust?

WHO CONTROLS WHO?
YOU CONTROL YOU!

You can control the way you feel!

You can control your Intention!

You can control your desire!

You get to decide how you act or react to how you feel...
about everything - including control.
You can only truly control you!

So what is it - that you can control that best serves you?

You can control only the choices you make - true?

And if those choices are of positive or negative - true?
TRUE THAT!

In Knowing that you **think** 60-70,000 thoughts a day -
with more than 90% of those thoughts being repeated daily
out of familiar habit...

Would you agree that it is time to pay attention to your thinking?
To understand - what you are creating in your everyday life experience - yes?

List 7 things you know you over-focus on daily.

1/

2/

3/

4/

5/

6/

7/

Your Thoughts Can Rule You OR You Can Rule your Thoughts...
Which Would You Rather Choose?

What of your 7 list can you choose to rule - rather than they rule you
& your emotions?

TO LISTEN IS TO BE SILENT!
TO BE SILENT IS TO LISTEN!

Are you listening?!

Are you?!

When your silent - you are - right?

Or Could you be busy listening to the chaos in your head?

If so - Then you are neither silent nor in listen mode.

Interesting fact -

Silent & Listen are spelled from the same letters.

I believe the message is clear in the afore mentioned - they work in tandem!

Word! 🩶

What is your **understanding** of yourself, of your partner,
of your family, (genetically related or not) -
even your friends?

Do you know or have even given it a 2nd thought?

Do you play the dice of **give, take & compromise** -
for the greater good of your commitments, friendships & relationships?

If not - why not?

Could it be that you are choosing ego directed behavior
& an attitude of sorts over understanding?

Do you agree that it takes effort on some level
to understand others?

Then isn't it about time you gave yourself this gift
of understanding?

Wouldn't you agree it is true that ...
understanding in this life experience, seems to be lost?
Are you feeling lost?

What are you losing out on in this life experience -
that you would like to acknowledge - with better, clearer understanding?

Can you add it to your to do list, give it some daily positive thought...
or add it to the bucket list of things... that you believe, will bring you closer
to experiencing your joy?

Understanding - can be the choice pathway to experiencing more joy 

LOVE

Who loves who? Do you love you?
You really, really should!

That warm hearted feeling, the contentment for self ...
that is much the same as the feeling you feel
when holding a brand new baby or puppy.

Why wouldn't you want this for you?
Your worth it! You really, really, are! Believe it & get with feeling it!

It's catching on - it really, really is!

Much the same way a smile to a stranger - has that knock on domino effect.

If you can make someone's day with that positive smile -
then why not make your own day great first!

It really, really, is quite catching!
Go ahead - do it - you got nothing to lose!
Happy Loving you day everyday 💞

Serve yourself first & then make that strangers day
& feel that
knock on
domino effect
in motion.

This is A form
of Powerful
Love 💗

What defines **LOVE** for you?

Did or Does your partner value the same?
Do you even know?

Is it or Was It Infatuation Attention that had or has a grip on you or your partner?

What were you or are you looking for?

Where you or Are you truly wanting to build a relationship of life long love?

Then - Where You or Are you compatible beyond infatuation?

Living together in some form of Harmony & Chemistry ...
is required would you agree?

When someone didn't want or doesn't want the same ...
Did you or Do you downward spiral into the depths of rejection?

While it can be quite normal to go this route -
based on the mind attaching 2 1/2 times more to the negative!
Ask yourself -
Why did you or do you want to be with someone who is showing you -
they do not align with you?

Ask yourself -
Was there or Is there a foundation strong enough to build upon?

Did they or Do they cheer you on - with your hopes & dreams?

Did you or Do you even discuss each others dreams with one another?
Did you or Do you understand or even know...
what it is - the other person was or is looking for in life?

So ask yourself...
What did you or can you learn from that or this relationship?

What was or am I attached to in that or this relationship?

What was or is my expectation / was or is it realistic?

Where you dating without determining exclusivity?

Where you or Are you committed to each other fully?

Ask yourself...
Where you or are you able to show your true authentic self?

Where you or Are you being realistic?
Can you be realistic about the love that was or is?

Did you or Do you set unrealistic expectations of others - even yourself?
Could Unrealistic expectations = inauthenticity of you or your partners true values?

The toughest part of any relationship is to :
Listen without defending & Speak without offending

As great as your parents or role models might have been ...
Did they or Do they show you - what a good or great relationship consists of?
What where you or are you willing to accept ...
that as you grew or grow & learn(ed) -
your expectations changed or change in friendships & relationships?

FRIENDSHIPS OF GOLD!

They say friendship is the golden thread that ties hearts together .

So spend it with those who mean the most to you 

As we learn to master speaking without offending

&

practice listening without defending……

we hope the golden thread holds strong unchanging the greatest parts of us that we share with one another

Life's experiences take us down pathways…
we sometimes have no business being on.

It is on such pathways…

We depend on
the golden thread
of friendship
&

The **Heart** is a super strong muscle of the human body - true?

Its function is essential to the human experience - true?

It has an amazing ability to mend itself repeatedly - true?

Loving bigger & better than it did previously - true?

So what do you do - for that heart to stay strong & thrive...
as it remains true to you?

Do you feed it what it wants & needs?
or
Do you shove in it only what your tongue desires to taste?

Do you know what your heart wants for you?

If your heart was running the mind body connection solely...
What would be on its daily menu?

Good nutritious food & water?
Some good walking exercise at minimum?
Breathing in good fresh air?
Someone to share your heart desires with?

All of the above - yes?

What do all of the above mean for you?

That you love your heart - true?

To love & care for your own heart is true self love - would you agree?

Do you agree - we go through broken hearted times?

But your heart does not stop working - does it?

It shows you how precious time can be - does it not?

Do you know what your heart aches for?

What it screams for?

Show your heart some Love & give it, what it needs to stay healthy - then let that love vibrate out, to feel that loving feeling, of sharing with the deserving!

So who is deserving of your sharing?

One who knows & shows your heart is deserving of sharing theirs with you too - true ?

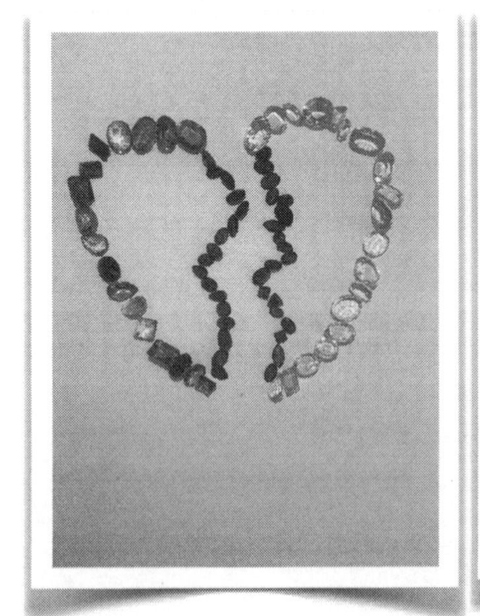
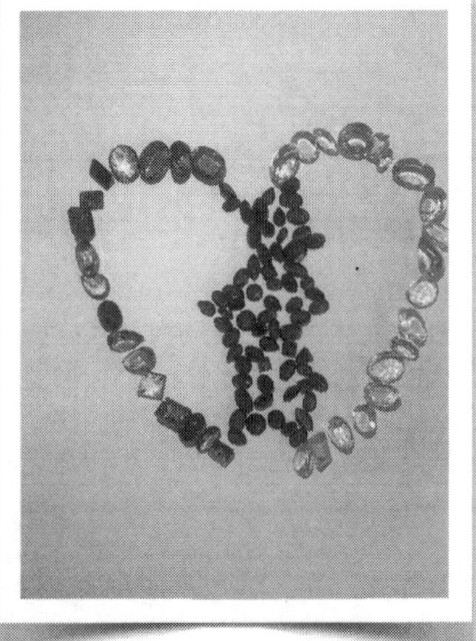

<u>Happiness</u> Is The Journey To Your Destination ❣

Do you have a destination in mind ...

just waiting for you to be brave & take that first step?

You can be as brave as you choose to be ...

because the choice is yours to make - true?

Believe in yourself & in turn - teach others...

they can believe in you too ❣

Be Brave ❣

Believe ❣

Enjoy that journey ❣

Build Your Heart Muscle ❣

IT IS A CHOICE TO GIVE ❣

IT IS A CHOICE TO

RECEIVE ❣

Are you giving **Love & Attention?**
Receiving Love & Attention?
or calling for (sometimes screaming for) Love & Attention?

What is it you want & need?

What is necessary & Why?

Would you agree that self love & appreciation are necessary?

What self love are you denying & why?

No matter your conception - you were created & born,
with your expectation of being adored, cared for & loved.

If for any reason this did not happen in a positive light -
make no mistake... it was nothing you did or didn't do!

It is the lack of capacity of those in charge of your younger you...
who are supposed to do the good **above** for you - true?
Maybe they could not for reasons - that really, no longer matter!
Only you can make these reasons matter to you...
by bringing such reasons into your present time.

If you are a parent -
In what capacity of love are you considering -
those you brought into the world or have the privilege to raise?

What truly matters is that any cycle of suffering ends with you...
breaking free of the cycle you found yourself in.
& understand this - **you are capable of all you want & need!**
But it does start with you giving to you first...
& acknowledging you are worthy!

List 7 things you are worthy of & why?

1/

2/

3/

4/

5/

6/

7/

In reviewing the above - can you now do this exercise
with someone you love & care for?

Can you write the 7 things you believe they need & why?
Meanwhile ... they can do the exercise of doing the same for themselves!
Then they can do it for you too - if they so wish!

What you will come to understand is that - there are some things ...
we just didn't know - due to everyones receiving & / or giving of love
to be very different to the next person.

But the fact that you now know -
what you have learned in this exercise ...
you are quite possibly able to love better - if not greater - than ever before!

LOVING YOU IS EASY
COS' YOU'RE BEAUTIFUL

LOVING YOU IS EASY
COS' YOU'RE ………………

LOVING YOU IS EASY
COS' YOU'RE ………………

LOVING YOU IS EASY
COS' YOU'RE ………………

LOVING YOU IS EASY
COS' YOU'RE ………………

LOVING YOU IS EASY
COS' YOU'RE ………………

LOVING YOU IS EASY
COS' YOU'RE ………………

Finish each of the above several started statements when looking at yourself & your qualities.
Then do it for your partner, child, relative, friend, co worker (s) ...
Anyone - that you feel for or have a connection with.

Loving from the heart is the only way forward!
It is for your greatest good & the world as a whole.

your

W - Worth

is

O - Obviously

inside

R - Remaining

well

T - Tucked

away

H - Hiding

from

Y - You - Yourself

You Are Worthy ❣

Look & Reach Inside ❣

It's Waiting For You To Decide...

You Are WORTHY ❣

THOSE 3 LITTLE WORDS

I LOVE YOU ❣

I DO ❣

DO YOU LOVE YOU?

Do you know what Love is?

What does it feel like?

Look like?

Can you touch Love?

Can You Imagine True Love? ❣

Love yourself first out of necessity because …

gaining your self worth is essential to …

one who needs - needs to navigate lifes roller coaster ride …

for a better experience ❣

It is your necessity!

Look in the mirror & see who looks back at you….

Describe what you see……

Compliment yourself!

You do have great qualities!

Show yourself some love 

you deserve it!

Tell yourself, why you are proud of you!

What beauty do you see & feel of yourself?

Did you fill yourself up with Self Love?

Yes!?

Now go show someone else - some of that Love & make their day too 

Because you can 

Because you are willing 

Because you are able

Remember to use those 3 little words 

I LOVE YOU - Luv Ya Man - Luvs Ya Babes - Luv ya Darl etc!

BECAUSE YOU CAN DECIDE ……… I AM WILLING / I AM ABLE 

As my friend Vanessa once said - "We choose who we give our love to" 

SO BE CHOOSY & BE WORTHY TOO ❣

E - ETERNAL

G - GROWING

O - OF

Do you feed your own **EGO?**

Does your ego require - or demand an all too familiar pattern -
to be fed externally?

What bruises your ego & why?

Do you avoid getting your ego hurt & bruised?

Do you realize that in the process of such -
you give your power up to something or someone else?

And so what responsibility to yourself are you giving up on & ...
to what or to who?

Do they (the what or who) have your best interests at heart -
both completely & unconditionally - just as you would for yourself?

If you had your best interests at heart -
then wouldn't you agree - that you would feed your own ego internally?
WITHIN ❣

DO YOU HAVE YOUR BEST INTERESTS AT HEART?
If not - why not?

What is seemingly in the way?

AWARENESS

What does Awareness mean to you?

What are you aware of?

Your wants…. Your needs… Your necessities?

Your loved ones wants & needs - or only necessities?

Your family & friends wants & needs - or only necessities?

Are you aware of the demands placed upon you?

Do you realize you have choices & can make better choices …
once you have an awareness of your ever changing surroundings?

Are your surroundings calming & enjoyable?

If not - why not?

You can choose your surroundings the same way you choose…
what to be aware of - true?

What is your CHOICE of
awareness?

Are you concerned enough…
to be well-informed &
aware of your choices?

Are you Happy or Unhappy?

Which are you? One or the other? Some of both?
What's your rhyme & reason?

Do you even know - or give attention to what they both feel like?

Does one feel more familiar than the other?

Does your happiness depend on someone else?
If so - who?
Why would you put that expectation on someone else?

Is this a pattern with you - in your life to date?

Can you just choose to decide - that happiness is a birthright?
How would that change the way you view your availability of choices...
in order to be happy - or happier in your here & now?

When walking down a street (in passing another person)...
most of us smile at a complete stranger which...
usually prompts the same action of reaction in return - true? (MOSTLY)

But - do we practice this in the home when being greeted
or greeting someone at the end of a busy day?

Are you guilty of treating strangers better than your nearest & dearest?
Do you even think or know why?
You do have the choice on what to think about & consider - true?

What can you choose to decide going forward?

Are you appreciating your happiness -
or letting unhappiness depreciate your life experience?

Are you Appreciating or Depreciating your preferences?

EITHER / OR?

Is your mind your **sickness** or your **medicine**?

Which do you focus on mostly … maybe always?

Which is dominant & why?

Some have it tough because of the way the body behaves …
bringing the attention to an issue - true?

I'm sure it is remembered … in that same mind & body -
how good it felt, it looked & maybe you even loved it - true?
It is that same body & mind - true?

Did it not just evolve through experiences & influences
of mostly your choosing?

So why not put on a tune you enjoy - that raises your vibration
& sooth yourself with all those great loving, looking, feelings
often enough - that your mind & body enjoys the excursion ❣

Then repeat, repeat, repeat ❣

Create any momentary scenario that feels so good …
so good that you want to keep reproducing OR
writing these small chapters …
because the moments of Joy it brings - are so worth it ❣

Joy is & can be your Medicine - if you choose it?

Your power lies in your mind ...
waiting for you to decide to Align ❣

So why not start enjoying your journey...
from where you are now -
on each & every day that arrives?

You are worth it & ... worthy of feeling Joy & Comfort -
if only in the mindful moments❣

If you can repeat, repeat, repeat this -
you will soon find you have arrived ...
at the place of soothing & experiencing
a form of beautiful Joy❣

SO WHAT'S YOUR FAVORITE SONG?
THE ONE THAT GETS YOU OUT...
OUT OF OF YOUR SEAT -
PHYSICALLY OR MENTALLY ❣

You can focus on the Sickness
or add this to your medicine ❣

GO GET IT ON
MY BUSY 🐝 FRIEND ❣❣❣

When we get **Sick or Ill** ...
we tend to focus on how bad it all feels -
while describing in detail to others every little thing ...
that is felt & understood around the sickness or illness.

& this process is repeated over & over again as people ask...
how we are doing - becoming quite the repetitive pattern.

So given the fact ...
that what we focus on - we get more of ...
Do you think we could feel better in such a pattern?
Difficult - true?

Maybe if it is just a passing bug that seems to be making the rounds!

But ... what if you choose not to dwell on the negative of...
your sickness or illness experience?
What could be your focus?
Wellness - right?

Do you think you are able to be **'greatful'** for all the things
that are right & well with your body?

In Knowing your wellness ... & the many parts of your body that function so well - regardless of the sickness or illness ...
Does your wellness seem to get lost or sidelined - in the chaos of repetition - dwelling only on sickness & illness?

Your brain is your operating system of your body
& it is its job to keep you alive / in survival mode - correct?

Then your feelings are the language of your body - true?

Your thoughts & their patterns with the feelings attached -
are what tell your brain what you want - true?

Then isn't it about time you decided -
what you want to focus on repeatedly?

& focus on feeling the good ...
maybe even those great emotions around your thoughts of focus...
so that...
your brain can produce more of that good feeling in your body.

CAN WE CHOOSE TO DECIDE...
THAT THE SIMPLER THINGS & SOLUTIONS ...
ARE A BETTER FOCUS?
MUCH BETTER THAN THE OVER FOCUS ...
ON PROBLEMS THAT ONLY HAVE DIFFICULT CHOICES ...
ALONG WITH DIFFICULT FEELINGS - TRUE?

WHAT COULD YOU BE APPRECIATING WHILE IN SICKNESS
& ILL HEALTH?

EG: I appreciate that my eyes get to see the beauty in all I have in my life!

I appreciate getting to experience nature with my senses.
(I am hearing, seeing, smelling, tasting & touching!)

I appreciate those who take the time out to make my life
simpler, easier to navigate, & feed my soul.

Wouldn't you agree - that regardless of ones sickness or illness...
We can still find joy in each day - beauty too ...
& experience so many wonderful things to be 'greatful' for?

& as for kindly enquiring to someone you know who is sick or ill ...
why not compliment them on how well they look, on a part of them
that is well!
Bringing their focus to their wellness is appreciating their wellness -
true?

HEALTH

(ingredient #1) - **H** Hope for better

(ingredient #2) - **E** Energy to do better

(ingredient #3) - **A** Ability to do better

(ingredient #4) - **L** Love of self

(ingredient #5) - **T** Take-Charge & do better

(ingredient #6) - **H** Happiness is being better

IN HEALTH - it often means caring for our elders - true?
But - does it mean we do everything for them?
Are they still capable of doing for themselves while you kindly supervise?
Even if it's just a thing or 2 ❣

Are you in the habit of responding
& speaking for them?

Your heart may be in the right place -
but - is it right to have their voice silenced?

What is healthier for their mind
& not just yours?

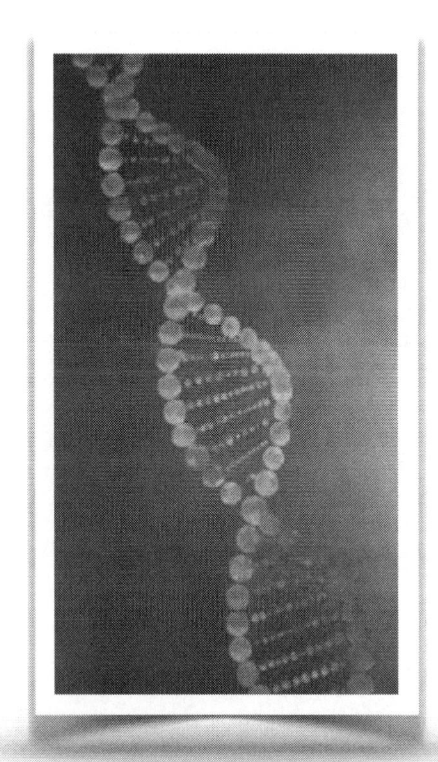

Wellness & So It Is

It's time to have Faith in my Mind & my Body

I give Myself Permission to Feel Good

Anything I Want IS Available to Me

I Have an Abundance of Wellness

I CHOOSE Well Being

I AM HEALTHY

I AM ENOUGH

And So It Is

Your heart holds love for you just waiting for you to connect 💗

There is more love inside that heart than you could ever imagine 💗

DO YOU GIVE YOURSELF **PERMISSION**?

Permission to be better, do better, feel better...
In your now - your day, your week, your month, your year, your life? ❣

You give permission up to others all the time ...
as you are guided to grow & learn from baby to child & teen etc. - true?

But, as an adult this permission becomes more personal to your
ME, MYSELF & I - true?

What permission do you give to yourself?

The permission to feel good, feel better, do better?

The permission to know & grow yourself into a brighter future?

The permission to do something greater than yourself?

THINK ABOUT IT ❣

What **permissions** will you consider & give to yourself?
In understanding that kindness starts with being kind to -
YOUR YOU, YOUR ME, YOURSELF & I FIRST!

🐝 KIND TO YOU 1ST & GIVE YOURSELF THAT PERMISSION ...
THAT NO ONE ELSE POSSIBLY TRUSTED YOU WITH -
BECAUSE - YOU NOW HAVE THE CHOICE ...
TO TRUST THIS PERMISSION TO YOURSELF ❣

PRISON or JAIL?

What type of prison do you find yourself caged in?

The one of the mind -
the self inflicted kind -
that keeps your you with a feeling that's mistakenly true -
& unkind to your you?
or
The one called the body - that can't work as designed?
With a bigger purpose for you & yours to find!

Maybe your in an actual cell box -
resulting from what was not a planned detox! (saved!)

Whatever your prison or jail may be...
Surely there's a bigger issue - at play for thee?!

Could it be your there as a result of your thinking -
Since everything begins & ends with an inkling?

Could it be you - being in there - has saved you again once more?
How could you not know - what it is ...
that the universe is saving you for?

Whether guilty or not ... from having not ...
your own best interests at heart!
Would you have known what ... your best interest(s) to be -
had you not been feeling a lot of I AM NOT?
The best thing for you - may be in your you...
As it awaits your you in trusting ...
your dearly divines belief in you too - you simply must just trust!

PUT THE BOOT ON THE OTHER FOOT

Put the boot on the other foot they said...

What foot & why?

What did you do ... that offended so true?

Offended who, when, where & how?

The one you took advantage of - unknowingly, but true!

Because you never thought of who, when & where -

when you did the how for you...

Making true - that boot fit - fit good on you!!!

If that was not you - then who fit that boot ?

You dear you!

Is True?

Did you consider

if that boot fit

who, when, where, how

& not just you?

Is **Grief** the Love that can no longer be placed -
upon a physical being (person) or thing -
that is due to the loss, inducing a form of **mourning**?

After all - it is a response to a loss of some kind of bond - true?

This tends to leave the mind & body in a connected turmoil...
many find difficult to navigate!

Could **Grief** be what we feel -
when we are feeling sorry for ourselves ...
because selfishly - we want them back at all costs?

Meanwhile ... What could it be costing you?
Your marriage, your relationship, your quality of life being sidelined!
Hold that thought!

Could it be we unknowingly punish ourselves on some level -
for still existing -
especially when the loss - was one that endured sickness, suffering or tragedy?

I believe yes - since grief can be beyond the emotional ...
such as feeling the effects physically -
often triggering some form of behavior -
& inducing some sort of domino effect.

For example: Someone choosing to drown the pain in alcohol or
numb it with a form of Self medicating.

Some say Grief has 5 Stages of mourning
Denial, Anger, Bargaining, Depression & Acceptance ❣

I'm sure if anyone has experienced loss, grief & mourning ...
it created an unfamiliar change ...
& so understand 1 or more of the above - true?

Most of us relate loss, grief & mourning to...
the death experience of a beloved person - true?

But isn't there many more subjects in life ...
grief can be experienced through too?

The loss of a pet...
the end of a chapter in your life ...
grieving the loss of an item with sentimental value placed upon it...
& the list goes on............

What is your loss & the list of issues that are related to it?

Considering all of this - do you believe you have a choice...
in how you would prefer to respond to loss, grief, mourning & change?

Would your loved one want you feeling this way repeatedly?

Do you prefer to remain in a reaction state &
it's continued domino effects?

For most of us - we do what we learned - correct?

But does it need to be true for you?

Can you choose to understand that there are many -
who feel equally at a loss over this death experience...
of a person, situation, chapter, reason or season etc.?

Can you choose to simply understand...
that all things come to an end...
at some point in time?

Can you also simply choose that death -
or an end of something is a part of the life experience?

& in knowing this ...
can one accept that while emotionally painful ...
we can still choose to celebrate all that was...
& is now a completed journey within the human experience?

Can you decide to cherish every thing, person, chapter, reason or season etc.
that brought you some form of learning, love, joy, happiness
& so on - yes?

Isn't this a wonderful acknowledgement of choice?

When it is your time to leave this present...
(whether it be life, an experience, relationship, chapter, reason or season) -
how would you want it to be celebrated?

Moving on should always be celebrated - no?

I like to believe that 'Moving on' -
is like moving up into a new class of wisdom 

'Moving on' does not mean to forget...
You can never forget the greatness of a life, of an experience,
of a relationship, a chapter, a reason or season.

& why would you want to forget ...
the experiences that make you - you today?

What can you choose to embrace, to celebrate & why?

My favorite thing to do when I lose someone or missing a loved one...
Is to play their favorite song or...

Listen to a beautiful song called **Dancing In The Sky**
By Dani & Lizzy

Here are the lyrics...

I DO NOT OWN ANY RIGHTS TO THE FOLLOWING LYRICS
I WISH TO SHARE THE BEAUTY OF THEM ONLY!

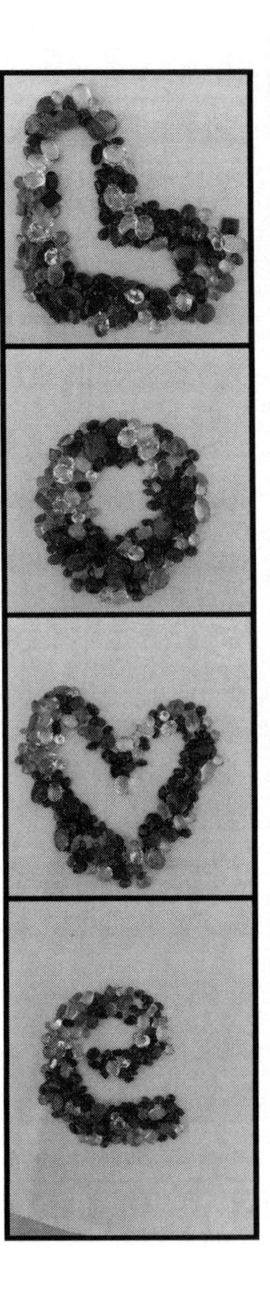

Tell me, what does it look like in heaven?
Is it peaceful? Is it free like they say?
Does the sun shine bright forever?
Have your fears and your pain gone away?

'Cause here on Earth it feels like everything
Good is missing since you left
And here on Earth, everything's different
There's an emptiness

Oh-oh, I
I hope you're dancing in the sky
And I hope you're singing in the angel's choir
And I hope the angels know what they have
I'll bet it's so nice up in Heaven since you arrived

So tell me, what do you do up in Heaven?
Are your days filled with love and light?
Is there music? Is there art and adventure?
Tell me are you happy? Are you more alive?

'Cause here on Earth it feels like everything
Good is missing since you left
And here on Earth everything's different
There's an emptiness

Oh-oh, I
I hope you're dancing in the sky
And I hope you're singing in the angel's choir
And I hope the angels know what they have
I'll bet it's so nice up in Heaven since you arrived
Since you arrived

Oh, oh
(What does it look like in heaven?) Yeah, yeah
Oh, oh, oh-oh
Oh-oh, oh
Oh, oh, I
I hope you're dancing in the sky
And I hope you're singing in the angel's choir
And I hope the angels know what they have
I'll bet it's so nice up in Heaven since you arrived
Since you arrived

Another Beauty is **GOODBYE By Kenny Rogers**
Here are the the lyrics...

I wanted you for life, you and me in the wind
I never thought there'd come a time that our story would end
It's hard to understand but I guess I'll have to try
It's not easy to say goodbye

For all the joy we share, all that time we had to spend
Now if I had one wish, I'd want forever back again
To look into your eyes and hold you when you cry
It's not easy to say goodbye

I remember all those great times we had
So many memories, some good, some bad
Yes and through it all, those memories will last forever

There's peace in where you are, maybe all I need to know
And if I listen to my heart, I'll hear your laughter once more
And so I have to say I'm just glad you came my way
It's not easy to say goodbye

GRIEF - LIFE CELEBRATION ❣

The newness of Grief throws us into a slow moving rollercoaster ride
with raw emotions & a very heavy heart.

We hold on for dear life it seems - all the while showing outwardly &
feeling numbness toward normal daily life interactions - we were once used to.

It's true nothing will ever feel the same because...
someone so significant in our lives, is no longer there to touch or respond to
us - the very way we often took for granted ❣

Their energy, spirit, love, legacy are with us forever &
we so want to celebrate this like we have never celebrated before.

Except, for the many - the hurt seems to cripple from doing this -
the way the loved ones lost ... hopes we can do!

So as time moves on & heavy emotions get familiar - so familiar -
that they are easier to carry with
us....

We move forward into
the celebration phase -
keeping the memory of our
lost loves alive in present time.

What a journey ❣

May our Beautiful Angels
be in peace & love ❣
& Thank-you for being
those bright guiding lights,
we so need, as we continue
our human experience.🖤

De L

We grow up seeing people pair up into **relationships** ...
& want that for ourselves too - true?

We get to know the feeling of infatuation, of companionship, of love,
of sharing & the making of a life together - creating experiences in unity!

Some of us growing up - only got to see the best times...
While some of us only felt the worst times - true?
But, regardless of what was & is seen or felt -
We idolized or idolize our parents in some which way, shape or form...
We wanted or want to keep their love & attention...
To please them...
& then we have a pattern many of us adopt as ours.
Maybe becoming a belief system...
Both religious & not!
Mostly not in this day & age (IMO).
Many of the behaviors we see are not of good or of good religious guided
upbringing (IMO).

All the above are our Perfect or not so Perfect examples of...
what a relationship is - regardless of its content.

& so what do we consider a good relationship?

More importantly - what do you consider a good relationship for you?

Define what a good, balanced, loving relationship is for you
& then become that ideal person for someone else!

What is the above defined as - for you?

For what you focus on - you can only get more of...
Assuming your emotions are attached to your defined wanted relationship -
Are they?

I Ask Because you must Believe to your core to Receive!

Are You Attracting What You Want?

What are you?

Happy, content, well, wealthy, abundant?

Whatever you tell yourself - is what is met!

Are you believing in what you want?

Do you acknowledge only what you want? Or

Do you acknowledge the lack of?

If the mind focuses 2.5 times more on the negative ...

Then why oh why would you give it energy time in your mind?

Habit of thought? Or

A lack of belief in yourself?

If you don't believe in you ....
Then how can others believe in you too?

Understand this!

Believing equates to receiving❣️

READ THAT AGAIN MY BUSY 🐝 FRIEND❣️

What kind of abundance are you swimming in -
in your present life situation?

Possibly the abundant lack of ...?

What kind of abundance would you prefer to be more dominant?
Money / love / happiness / joy?

What can you safely say you are abundant in?

YOUR THOUGHTS FOR SURE - true?

So why not tell yourself some better feeling thought's?

If you can worry - you can imagine ❣

True? SO TRUE ❣

So imagine abundance in all forms for your greater good!

Believe in your thoughts - enough to delete the 'lack of' vocab
& emotion from your mind ❣

Keep thinking those good thoughts - until those thoughts become your beliefs ❣

Positive Abundance is yours to believe in ❣

To Believe is to Receive ❣

YOU CAN Master your thoughts into abundance for your greatest good - if you choose!

Be patient - it takes repetition & time my busy 🐝 friend ❣

TRUSTING

T - Trusting
R - Responsibly
U - Unbelievably
S - Senses
T - Tenderness

Do you **Trust** easily ?

Do you or can you trust yourself to be **Responsible**?

Do you or can you act **Unbelievably** well with the trust invested in you?

Do you use your **Senses** to guide you?
(hear, see, smell, taste, & touch)

Do you treat the trust in you with the **Tenderness** it deserves?

Trust yourself & others will sense they can trust you too

The yellow butterfly

is associated with

clarity, confidence,

power, enlightenment,

energy & humility ❣️

CAN YOU RELATE?

What clarity have you achieved?

What confidence have you gained?

What power are you feeling?

Are you enlightened?

What energy are you vibing with?

Are you modest & humble in your daily life?

ENVIRONMENT

What does your personal environment look like?

Is it positive or negative?

Are you surrounded with people who gossip, complain & blame others?

While you may love & care for these individuals -
Does their energy affect you & your thinking?

Of course it does 

or

Do you have feelings of always being in the lack of ...
in your personal environment?

What are you truly lacking?

Do you know?

Observe your personal environment
&
understand why you are not your best friend yet

It is a process

And it can start any time you choose you are worthy ...
of the environment you desire

Is your environment fun & beautiful -
if only on an excursion in your imagination?
Is your environment with close connections?
If not - why not?

Do you have a **Connection** to those that bring out the best of you or those that remind you of the worst moments you once endured?

For the many it is some of each or at lot of one or the other!

For the "lucky" (as one would say) - it is mostly a positive experience from an attitude of appreciation on some level.

What kind of connection do you want or simply prefer without limits?

Emotionally connect to your answer above & describe in detail as you feel these good feelings expand.
For what you focus on - you will always get more of!

So it is with you to decide - if you want to deem yourself "Lucky" from here on in - telling yourself the following...

I'm so lucky - everything always works out for my greatest good.
OR
write your own phrase that suits you!

You have a choice to Choose wisely -
who you connect with or remain connected to...
when it comes to your well-being - true?

So I ask you - What connections are you choosing & why?

Aren't you so lucky, you get to choose which connections you keep - knowing it's for your greatest good?

What are you creating in your life?

Do you create with purpose & on purpose?

If not - why not?

You have the choice to decide to accept what others create in
& around your life - true?

Wouldn't you rather decide for you - yourself?
What do you want to deliberately & intentionally create?

Focus on the fun of it - you are worth it!

It may well be more beneficial to you & yours?

Think of that choice - it's yours to make - true?

Is it more important - to keep up with the Jones's of your world
with the pressures that come with such?
OR
Is it more important to feel - you are being true to you?

Assuming, you know you...
& understand when you feel content on your journey of Joy

Following your hearts desire - is an experience we are all worthy of

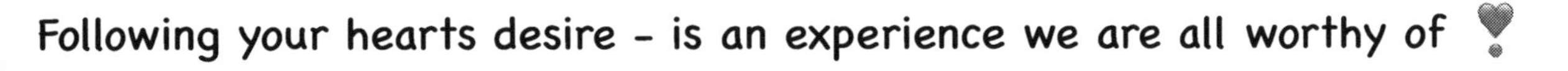

Ask yourself ...
Do you want to choose your worth & then create it?
This choice is yours

WHAT ARE YOU ADDICTED TO?

What emotions are you addicted to?

The ones you keep repeating...
without any notion of self control?

Does it serve you or hinder you?

Do you like this addiction...
or is it just so familiar that it feels so normal?

Is this ok?

Is it An easy pattern of an emotional response?

Is the deep pain still evident in present time?

How long have you been addicted?

Do you want to control your addictive behaviors & emotions?

You can choose to change your thoughts

& change your emotional response -

& behaviors in the process❣

Repetitions of thought are yours to master - if you wish!

What is of most **Importance** to you in order to live your best life?

( ) Is it Love? why?

( ) Is it career? why?

( ) Is it money? why?

( ) Is it attention? why?

( ) Is it happiness? why?

( ) Is it joy? why?

OR

All of the above?

In what order or priority?
(Number them & re-read them in your priority order often)

Can you define each of the afore mentioned
to **live your best life?**

Reread your definitions & come up with more emotional descriptive words of each - In understanding that as you focus on these emotions...
they will expand!
For what you focus on - you will always get more of!
So what is it - you are choosing to focus on?

YOUR GOAL IS...?

YOUR GOAL IS WHAT?

Is it for your greater good?

Is it a Want, Need or Necessary?

Do you care enough to know the difference of the above?

Does your goal involve caring?

Does it involve experiencing Joy in some form?

Will your goal involve Self Belief?

Or

Is your goal orientated in the hopes...
it would have others believe in you?

If you don't believe in you ...
then how can you expect others to believe in you too?

You must Believe to Receive!

Read that again ❣ You must Believe to Receive ❣

Heads up parents ❣ Your kids must Believe to Receive ❣

Are you leading by example by believing in them too?

SUCCESS

S - Silently

U - Undergo

C - Careful

C - Calibration in

E - Every

S - Single

S - Situation 

Success requires Careful Calibration on some level - true?

What is it you find yourself carefully calibrating to?

What does **Success** mean to you?
Love? / Money? / Career? / House? / Car?

Can you describe - how success feels for you?

What of your Successes from your childhood can you acknowledge,
that got passed over by your care givers?

Do you believe your parents, guardians & caregivers thought nothing much of
it - because, they knew you were destined for greater?
(This is a Likely possibility)

Many of those who raised or raise us don't or didn't have much
of a capacity, to give positively or even often -
sadly ... but likely due to lacking in their own experiences.
or Were - maybe are too in their head worrying about this or that -
keeping them out of that present moment.
Remember they were & are capable of being faulty humans too ❣

You may have the capacity of a bath tub or an ocean -
whereas someone else may be or have been the capacity of ...
a worn out dish rag. (sad but true!)

What do you believe your success capacity to be?

And what success capacity are you or did you grow or are growing up with?

Your belief in your answer works for you -
whether it is positive or negative -
because if you keep thinking it... it is your pattern of belief!

What you give attention to - you will always get more of!
SO......Does this belief come from you or another influence?
Again, I ask - what does success mean for you?

Are you Choosing & Losing out due to **Fear**?

What do you fear & why?

Do you even know?

Do you know you can buy into the fear or face & conquer it -
taking away the control fear has over you?

WHAT FEAR IS HOLDING YOU BACK FROM BEING THE BEST YOU CAN BE?

WHO HOLDS THIS POWER OF FEAR OVER YOU?

DO YOU KNOW - YOU DO!?

IT IS YOUR CHOICE TO USE IT OR LOSE IT (IT BEING YOUR POWER)
TO WHOMEVER OR WHATEVER YOU ARE CHOOSING TO GIVE YOUR POWER TO!

I challenge you to list 7 things you fear daily, weekly, monthly, yearly -
& face them, understand them & figure out your why!

1/

2/

3/

4/

5/

6/

7/

WHAT ARE YOU PLUGGING INTO?

Do you know?
Or
Know why?

The Familiar Habit -
Because it pleases someone else or
serves some kind of purpose?

If something needs electricity -
do you plug into the electrical socket - yes - true?

If you are sick - can you choose to plug into wellness?

If you feel irritated - can you choose to plug into patience?

If you worry - can you choose to plug into peace?

Pay attention to what you are plugged into - that brings you negative feelings & choose to only plug into - that which brings more ease & flow in all you require.
Those moments of happiness & joy... that bring on more of that happy, joyful momentum - should be of your choosing

You are worthy of your choices -
because you are only worth - what you choose to plug into

READ THAT AGAIN

CHOOSE YOUR WORTH -
BY KNOWING YOUR CHOOSING & WHAT YOUR PLUGGING INTO

You can own all your own **Experiences** - true?

Do you stand in your own **Truth**?

Clean or dirty - good & bad experiences are all yours, with continuous choices to learn from those experiences - true?

But - are you choosing to learn from every experience -
regardless of the negative or positive root?

You are not your past - unless you keep bringing it into the present time.
Is this what you could be doing?

So ask yourself - what are you constantly bringing & re-experiencing in ...
your present time from the past? (NOTICE 'THE PAST' NOT 'YOUR PAST')
(We all do it until we learn that we don't need to!)

Every day is a new day - a new beginning - a day for new experiences,
new learning curves & new teachings - true?

So What experiences will you decide to allow yourself each new day?

What experiences will you let your nearest & dearest see, feel, hear, taste & touch - through you & because of you ...
through your actions, reactions or your storytelling?

Do you let yours (your nearest & dearest) learn through their own process when the possibility arises?
or Do you cut that learning off at the knees ... doing this & that for them?

If so - what are you teaching them?
That you do not trust - they can learn to do for themselves? POSSIBLY ❣
There is nothing wrong with explaining or showing them ...
this is what you learned - how, when & why it has worked for you - true?

It all comes down to you choosing - what experiences serve you for the greatest good of you & yours!

Did someone in your life lead by **Example** by being a positive role model for you?

That role model could be anyone you saw do something ...
something you appreciated or simply witnessed on some level of Aw!
(A parent, relative, friend, famous person, stranger - so many possibilities!)

We all see or witness negative role models in our environment sadly!
But it is what we do with that information that impacts us greatly.
We can let it impact us negatively or positively!
By simply choosing to adopt this behavior as acceptable or not - true?

The way to know how it impacts you is to recognize how it makes you feel along with your action of reaction!

Did you ever look up to someone famous who was one of your role models?

What did they teach you?

Where you affected positively or negatively?

Are you repeating what you learned?

If not - why not?

Can you be a good role model?

Do you want to be a good role model?

What can you model positively?
(eg. attitude of happiness, attitude of appreciation, attitude of taking it all in your stride, etc. etc. etc.)

The Question is...
What example or examples - do you choose for you & yours & why?

Greater Good

When you give more - you get more!

What you focus on expands - literally!

So do yourself the best favor you could give yourself ...

& focus on the greater good of yourself!

For the Greater Good of those nearest & dearest to you too!

After all they do love you - true?

Smile - because you can...

& watch that knock on domino effect begin!

It catches on & on & on!

So give more - to get more!

Focus on the good & watch it expand!

Go on - give it your all .... THE GREATER GOOD OF YOU

FOR THE GREATEST GOOD OF YOU, ONE & ALL 

What kind of **Attitude** are you waking up with each & every day?

Are you thinking about what you dread each day...
inducing those feelings of anxiety?

Are you racing through in your mind, everything that is on your agenda - before you even get out of your bed?

If so - then its not a wonder why your so tired of feeling this way!

You just took your mind through a whole days journey in minutes - while feeling all those feelings about the day ahead.

Yet you wonder why your knackered! (shattered!)

You also wonder why your days feel so long!

Are you waking with an **attitude** of lacking in something?

This can be all so consuming - leading to thoughts & feelings of **"Why me"** which often translates to **"what am I doing wrong?"** or **"why am I not worthy?"**

It's time to remember every morning - what you can be 'greatful' for!

What are you 'greatful' for?
What can you find appreciation in or for?

This may be a difficult - even challenging thought to focus on at first - but with practice comes momentum &...
with momentum there comes confidence.

The confidence in knowing you can **choose your attitude** any day, any time, on any subject, for any reason you choose.

For **your attitude dictates** whether you let something in or not - that which does or does not serve you - true?

APPRECIATION!

A - Acknowledge

P - Pure

P - Perfection

R - Real

E - Exceptional

C - Creation

I - In

A - All

T - Things

I - I

O - Openly

N - Nourish

My Appreciation acronym

YOUR POTENTIAL!

Do you have faith...
in your own potential?

We all possess it ❣

Many of us don't give it a thought....

Why is that?

What do you have faith in...
& why ?

Your potential deserves some attention -
would you agree?

It is unlimited until you decide

you are limited.....

So where is your faith in you?

Is it in your unlimited

potential ? ❣

DO YOU PRAY?

Why do you pray?
Many of us were shown how to - true?

Does it serve a purpose - that is true to you?

Do you have faith in who you pray to?

Do you have faith - in the praying that you choose to do?

Many of us are taught that we should have a certain prayer position, a certain way of approaching, addressing - maybe even dressing when we pray to whom we have chosen as our highest power - **Our Dear Divine** - true?

Could it be - so it would be recognized - who worships who?

Does it matter who or how you worship since everyone & everything comes from an energy source - that same energy source that created all?

It should only matter to you - true?

Are you always asking for something in your prayers?

Do you ever pray in appreciation for the human life lessons &
the freedom to choose these many 'choosings'?

Do you pray on purpose & with purpose?

Prayer is said to be the most powerful channel of communication 

What matters is - that you have your one on one connection to your Dear Divine / higher power - whoever & however that is chosen to be

DIVINELY YOU

Are We The Divine
With Our Inner Guide
Living In A World
That Can Deadly Divide?
Simply Defining
Who, When & How
We Are To Be
With Who, When & Where!

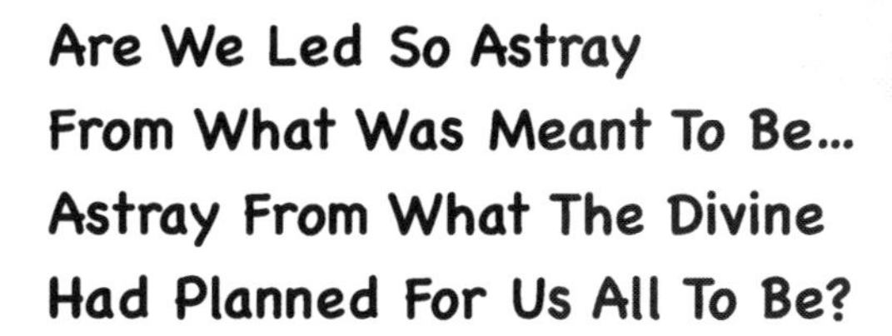

Are We Led So Astray
From What Was Meant To Be...
Astray From What The Divine
Had Planned For Us All To Be?

Someone Else's Planning
Means Banning More & More....
It's Sad - Yes It Is
To Get Left Behind Once More.

As They Ban The Free Will
Of The Kind & The Law
Only The Good - Yes the Good
Can Truly Adore
Those That Are Kind
To Us All -
One & All!

The Divine Will Conquer
The Free Will To Be
To Act & React...
In A World Meant For Thee!

A World Of Great Choices...
Choices To Act & React!
With Trusting Each Other
Not Seemingly Lost with THAT!.

From One To The Other
Undermining True Trust
Seems To Be The New -
The New - New Must!
By Those We Absolutely Cannot
& Will Not Trust!

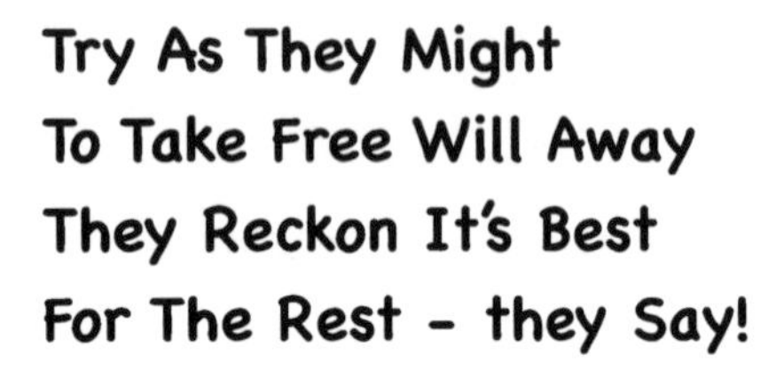

Try As They Might
To Take Free Will Away
They Reckon It's Best
For The Rest - they Say!

Yet The Many Believe -
That We Should Just Be...
As The Giving Way
Will Get Wider To Thee!

To The Most Unpopular Ideas
That My Dears
We Need Not - Never Ever Trust
Do you Trust What Your Ears
That Which - Brings Only Fears?

We Are All The Divine
With The Inner Guide Of All Joy
That Defeats & Deletes Wrong Purpose
Making Room For More Joy!

This be So Right
For True Reasons Of You
The Goodness, The True
Divinely Installed
To Your Inner Winner You!

And So
Who Are We
As A Divine Baby?
That Was Born Equipped
With Purpose To Be...

To Be Who We Feel
So Good Just To Be...
On This Journey Through Life
Discovering Our We.

The We Is Our Connection
To The Divine & Inner Guide
Looking For Love
In Our Purpose & Why?

And So Who Are We
When Connected To
The Divine & Inner Guide

The Vibrational You?

We Fill Up With Love
& Flow Over With Joy
Not looking Behind
Like A Thief Does
When Stealing Our Joy?

We Fill Up With Love
Because It Aligns With Our We
Instilling Much Joy
Experiencing Our Thee ...

The Inner Me Guide
That is so Great & Divine
Your Inner Loving YOU
Dear YOU - Dear Divine!

By De🐝 L.
June 11th 2023

D - DEVOTION
I - IN
V - VARIOUS
I - INDIVIDUALS
N - NEVER
E - ENDING ❣️

E	-	EVERYTHING
T	-	THAT
E	-	ENERGY
R	-	REACHES
N	-	NATURALLY
A	-	AIDS
L	-	LOVINGLY

'GREATFUL'

I am sure you have noticed my spelling of this word - changes up the position of some of the letters. Because, **I choose to believe** it was spelled mistakenly :0)

This word is positive - yet when you break down the "correct" spelling of this word - one can only envision a grate that is full.

Eg: Grates are used in many systems to catch the rain water run off - but to keep out the crap that often flows - with this water. (leaves, trash & the like that we ignorant humans discard so carelessly)

In any case, I believe the positive word now becomes a negative - being full of crap!

'Greatful' = Full of Greatness
A better representation of the word - would you not agree?

So when we are **'greatful'** for something ...
we are in **appreciation** of the subject - either for its existence or for the lesson we learn from the subject being **'greatful'** for.

An Attitude of Gratitude is how the many phrase it!

I prefer an Attitude of Appreciation myself.

Ask yourself - What am I 'Greatful' for?
What or whom do I Appreciate?

Then let your 'greatful' for - be known - for if they don't hear it or feel it with an action from you - how do you expect them to know that you are **'Greatful'** or **Appreciate** them?

WOKE

W - Wake up ❣

O - Open your heart ❣

K - Kindness works best ❣

E - Eagerly help your fellow man ❣

If your awake - then you can choose to pay attention with an open heart as you show kindness ...

Such eager actions alone help your fellow man!

Production of this frequency holds a positive value.

Be the real 'woke' people ❣

JOYOUS ME!

J - Judge

O - Only

Y - Your

O - Own

U - Unique

S - Senses

M - My

E - Emotion ❣

WHAT TICKLES YOU?

What tickles you & knocks on that door called Joy?

Do you even know?

A Long forgotten maybe?

When is the last time Joy opened that door
& you felt that tickle?

Y'know the one - the one that gave you that wide smile, that bright eyed look, that giggle, the feeling that felt good as the negative fell away - if only for a moment.

Y'know, if you find & review those moments & get busy enjoying, while remembering that joy - you might just feel enough joy - to be that joy at someone else's door.

Be that domino effect - that chain reaction of action.....

For Joy holds a key to a wide smile, a bright eyed look, a giggle & all things positively good - for the greater good ❣

Oh what JOY ❣

JOY ❣ JOY ❣ JOY ❣

WANT TO CHANGE YOUR LIFE?

Change your thinking

Catch your negative thoughts & ...

Opt for a better feeling thought

Changing your thinking...

Changes your feelings...

When you change your feelings positively & repeatedly...

The tip of Joy emerges!

Joy attracts more Joy!

It's vibration is all unto itself 

Making Joy familiar changes your life 

What others **THINK** of you is really non of your business!

Their thoughts are their thoughts - not yours!
& you cannot control what someone decides to think about you - true?

As we grow... we care what our parents & guardians think - true?
They are our guiding lights! (or should be)

But, do we need to believe in someone else's opinion?

We tend to value this, since we look up to our elders - true?

For many of us - it is not until a major life event -
do we realize what matters - which, is our own opinions of ourselves!

Our thoughts - are what we need to begin to understand, along with the emotions - that we attach or have attached to them!

Emotions are the story telling guiding system - true?
Are you listening, to this story telling system - that you allow to be repeated?

Ask yourself - if you are kind to yourself ❣

Ask yourself - if you are coming from a place of love in your thinking ❣

Are you really punishing the person you hold a **GRUDGE** towards
or ...
Could you be punishing yourself?

You are likely punishing yourself, because you are mad ...
Mad that you allowed yourself to be hurt ...
When you feel hurt it means you care!
& it's likely you thought highly of the hurters opinion - more than your own...
Otherwise why would it hurt?

A hurt that continues to hurt every time you visit that memory - true?

Every time you feel hurt emotions attached to a memory ...
you are likely feeling it somewhere in your body!

This stress on the body gives good breeding ground for disease to creep in...
Disease - means your body is experiencing a Dis-Ease!
It's uncomfortable!
It's troubling!
It's self destructive!

What you focus on - **you will always get more of** - true?

(getting it yet?)

So why focus on grudges & get more of the same in return?
(Along with the negative emotional luggage or baggage that is attached)

If someone dropped their grudge against you - how would you respond?
Is standing firm in your grudge better for your well being?
or
Could it be - you are scared to allow a hug to replace the grudge...
because it might just happen all over again?

Is it not worth the chance, the risk - in order to release...
Release the breeding ground that lets dis-ease creep into?

The Choice is Yours My Busy Friend

What can you **Let Go** of because you truly don't **Let It In**?

Is it right to hold onto, when deep down - you really don't want to?

What do you need to let go of ...
because letting it in - would not serve you?
or
Would it - actually serve you?

When you let someone in - do you give all of you?

Scared to?
Scared of what & why?

What experience brought this lack of trust in yourself & your judgement?

Does this experience belong in your present...
or
is it an echo of your past?

Is it worth letting it in & trusting it will be worth the journey...
for however long it may last?

If you don't try - you don't know - true?

Trust in yourself - to make a judgement - for your greatest good...

Trust in the journey un-scared of it's destination!

Trust the experience of - letting it go or letting it in!

Trust you can experience the experience...

For your Greatest Good

WHAT'S YOUR FREEDOM?

Your freedom depends on your choices 

How wisely you choose - is your freedom of choice 

Your freedom depends on your responses 

You have the freedom to choose your action.....

You have the freedom to choose your reaction.....

You are free to choose your choices -
Regardless of your surroundings....

Is your choice your choosing of an action or reaction...
that you blame on your surroundings?

Read that again

My busy Friend,
What are you choosing to Blame ... & why ...
when you have the Choice to Choose your kind of Freedom? 

WHAT IS YOUR FREEDOM?
ARE YOU & WILL YOU DECIDE TO CHOOSE ...
WHAT FREEDOM MEANS FOR YOU & WRITE IT INTO YOUR NOW?

De L

DIET is often related to food - but it is not just what we eat...
it is everything we consume - internally & externally.

Some say 'We are what we eat!' This will ring true as the body ages -
you will see
Changing familiar patterns are harder the longer they have been in practice.
Many of us have learned to eat to taste - instead of eating to maintain :0(

So - what are you eating more of?
Could you be eating less of something?
& more of something else - more beneficial?

Are you thinking in terms of your greatest good?
Are you someones example or role model?
Do you think - what they see is what they will do? DID YOU?

What else are you consuming?
What do you watch?
Beautiful heartwarming shows & movies?
Action style with a happy ending?
or Violent, aggressive, negative behaviors - that are all too real?
What emotions are you igniting when you consume the above?

What are you choosing to listen to & why?
Good feeling music - with words that ring true?
Heavy & deep music - making you feel more of the same - heavy & deep - or
could it be that you feel heavy & deep - so this music feels totally familiar?
Are any of these choices a reflection of your busy chaotic mind?
or some kind of other emotional connection?

What are you reading up on or not reading at all?
What is your **goal** in consuming the subject of focus?
Do you enjoy what has your attention?
Or - are you simply consuming what's up in your face on social media???

What are you choosing?

You do have free will to choose what you expose yourself to ...
& consume - true?

For some of you -
your parents & guardians may have done or be doing your choosing for you - for a brief time in your life.
One hopes they have your best interests at heart!

What company are you keeping?

Whoever is available & around?

Life long friends & family?

Do they have your best interests at heart?

Do they care - really care, or just enough to pacify themselves & you too?

When in school - parents often advised or advised you to hang out with the straight A students - true?
Why do you think that is?

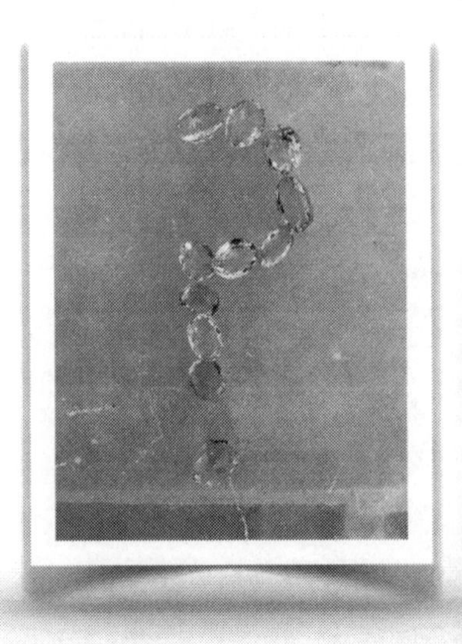

What are you drinking?

Do you know you are supposed to drink a minimum of several ounces of water upon waking?

Several more times in the day... & again before resting!

Do you know why?

Do you realize that the many times when we feel hunger -
we are actually hungry for water?

Without water our energy is poor!
Without water our foods carrying essential vitamins ...
cannot make it to their inner body part destination on time.

The foods we should enjoy are the ones that supply the body with the nutrients needed before the nutritional value expires.

If you put chewed up food in a pipe without water -
it will stick to the sides - correct?
This is what you do to your body when you eat -
without having sufficient water first.

Farting is not just from fiber...
it is most likely from foods stuck in your pipes - creating gases!

It is also possible that you have an overgrowth of candida.
This has you craving sugars in the many forms...
as well as preservatives & yeasts.

Healthy?
ABSOLUTELY NOT!

Adopting the **'everything in moderation'** is the least you can do for you & yours - would you agree?

I CHALLENGE YOU TO FIGURE OUT WHAT IT IS THAT YOU WANT, YOU NEED & IS NECESSARY FROM THE DIET THAT YOUR LIFE HAS IN IT!

TO KNOW WHAT IT IS THAT YOUR MIND & BODY NEEDS FROM YOU - FOR YOUR GREATEST GOOD - IT IS VERY IMPORTANT ❣️

WHAT ARE YOUR WANTS & WHY?

WHAT ARE YOUR NEEDS & WHY?

WHAT ARE YOUR NECESSITIES & WHY?

WHAT CAN YOU DELETE OR INTRODUCE THAT WILL BE OF BENEFIT TO YOUR MIND & MY BODY?

A diet only means restriction if you are only familiar with fast foods, fried foods, sugar saturated food & drinks - with the many preservatives etc.

Challenge yourself to a wellness diet - not just with food - but what you consume in experiencing - through watching, reading, listening & the likes. etc.

If you want to feel better - then you will simply choose to do better...
1 step at a time!

Making it Familiar EQUALS Making it Easier ❣

Would you expect the transportation of your choice …
to be ok on sugary liquids & dirty oil? NO!!
Then why would you expect your personal vehicle - (your body)
to work well without the correct fuel & fluids?

Make a list of all the things you consume in abundance
rating them with a scale of 1-10.
1 being of least value to you & your overall well-being.
10 being of great value to you & your overall well-being.

Then hi light what it is you would like to intake more of to support your mind
& body, as well as its functions!
Your diet intake is ultimately your choice!

D - DELIBERATE

I - INTERVENTION

E - ETHICALLY

T - TRUSTED

We are all in a **MOOD** of sorts day in / day out!
Spelled backwards is DOOM - coincidence?
But, are you in a stable mood - that serves you?
Is it one that is preferred?

Do you pay attention to what you are feeling?

Do you over focus on your moods (Dooms) ...
enhancing all the emotions attached to them?

Did you know that staying in a healthy hydrated state -
actually helps keep your moods more balanced ... more + ?

A mood is a temporary state usually instigated or
enhanced by your environment -
possibly a person, thing, situation or memory revisited &
your interpretation of being on the receiving end - true?

What moods OR Dooms do you consistently experience & why?
Some of the following can be experienced both positively & Negatively - true?
Add a + or - besides the moods you experience
Add a double + or - if you know the why ❣
(you are getting to know your you ❣)

Happiness	Sadness	Fearful	Angry
Joy	Depression	Alarmed	Aroused negatively
Contentment	Misery	Astonished	Annoyed
Serenity	Gloom	Afraid	Excited
Ease & Flow	& Doom	Tension/Stress	Delighted
Relaxed	Boredom	Frustration	Enthusiastic
Calm	Tiredness	Disgust	Glad
Sleepy			

It is natural for us to experience negative emotions "THE DOOMS" to the
things that scare us, make us nervous or sad.
While mostly the opposite is true... for positive emotions...
that bring out mostly happiness & joy - even reaching for more of the same.

Stress is something we experience when we react
to a physical or emotional tension - true?
Being nervous, frustrated or angry are often partnered with stress!

Anxiety can be the result emotion from a physical issue -
such as Blood Pressure.

It can be induced through thought alone - as the brain cannot
tell the difference between thought & reality!
(your brain is your operating system)
(your mind / imagination form & hold your thoughts)

Avoidance of certain things - is often a coping mechanism
for the worriers of the world.
Worriers have great imaginations - but have not learned yet
to utilize their imagination for their complete benefit!

Our minds are much the same way a story writer uses word choices
to set the stage, imagery & tone for the reader.
You can set your own stage & imagery as well as tone ... each & every day
if you **choose** to.
Of course it may take practice ...
but, isn't this with everything in this life of our human experience?
We can reset as we rest & start each day ... as a new day repeatedly - true?

If we experience something that has become engraved as a pattern
& that attached emotion is repeatedly triggered -
you are now on an autopilot reaction of action.

Knowing how a pattern is created ...
Can you not use this & your imagination to your advantage ...
developing a pattern that serves you & your greatest good?

SO SET YOUR OWN MOOD! MASTER YOUR THOUGHTS! NOT YOUR DOOMS!
SET YOUR OWN STAGE EVERY DAY & FOLLOW YOUR JOY

IMAGINE

I	-	I
M	-	Maintain & Manage
A	-	Awareness
G	-	Growing
I	-	Inside
N	-	Naturally
E	-	Everyday

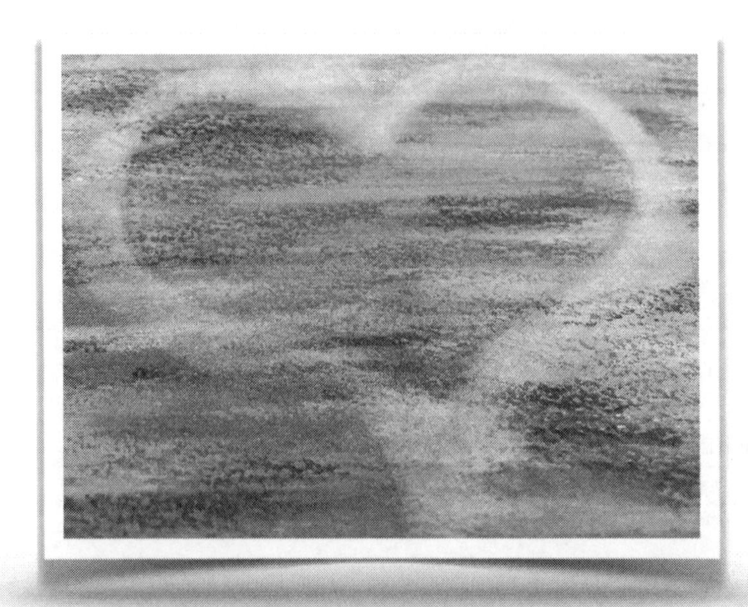

ARE YOU SURVIVING OR THRIVING?

HOW ARE YOU SURVIVING? HOW ARE YOU THRIVING?

OR, WHAT WHERE YOU DOING WHEN YOU WERE THRIVING THAT ...
YOU ARE NOT DOING WHEN YOU ARE SURVIVING?

When people ask "how are you?" - what do you answer?
SURVIVING?!

Do you want to keep Surviving or do you want to be Thriving?

What would you be doing if you where Thriving?
READ THAT AGAIN!

What could you be hanging onto -
that is preventing you from moving forward?

What do you need to let go of -
that stands in your way of Thriving?

Challenge yourself to write as many things, that you feel,
you need to conquer - so you can keep reaching that Thriving Status.

What of your list - can you simply choose to let go of & practice life without?

It is your **choice** to be in Surviving or Thriving...
because you ultimately make decisions for you - true?

WHAT ARE YOUR POISONS?

CAN YOU REPLACE THEM WITH YOUR PASSION?

What poisons your human experience?

FEAR? GREED? IGNORANCE?

Whatever negative habits OR hurdles you have ...

OWN IT & THEN CHOOSE TO TRASH IT!!!!!

MAKE BETTER CHOICES!!!

CHOOSE to be HAPPY!

CHOOSE to be 'GREATFUL'! (Full of Greatness!)

CHOOSE to be LOVE!

WHATEVER YOU GIVE MORE OF ❣

YOU GET MORE OF ❣

CHOOSE THE JOY ❣

CHOOSE THE LOVE ❣

🐝 **LOVE**

This Photo is credited to my life long friend Shirley Gamble, Australia

You Know!

Are you meditating or medicating?

Which choice is best for you?

Meditation is simply choosing a better feeling - along with mindful breathing - as the mind quiets!

Medicating is choosing to ignore & numb what's best for you & those around you!

It is a choice to take a breath, find a good feeling & raise your vibration in an instant!

It is a choice to believe in yourself ...

& focus on appreciating all that you are.

You know how amazing you can be!

You know you want to shine!

You know it feels good to make good choices.

Make it, be it, see it, feel it, love it &

love your choice by making it familiar 

READ THAT AGAIN MY BUSY FRIEND

What are you **Fearing** & why?

Is it the thoughts, actions & reactions of others toward you?

Has someone bullied you - or even threatened to?

Do you believe - they have the right to do this to you?

Is your self worth less than your actual worth?

Those you fear learned this behavior somewhere!

Hurt people - Hurt people!
Read that again!!!

Why you wonder!

The Why is their issue!
It only becomes your issue ...
if you constantly bring or allow that fear into your present ...
which then presents the same emotions attached to them - True?

When you fear something from the past & give it your attention...
You give it life in the present!

It is something you experienced & can let go of -
if you choose!

Does a past experience still induce emotions that don't serve you?

Do you know Why?

When you talk about it in the present - you give focus to the energy it held
& enable it to expand in your now!
Maybe it's time to write & release those fears!

Write it out of your system in past tense &
as you see the words reach the paper -
recognize they are no longer inside of you!

Then comes the choice you need to make...
Are you ready to let it go?
Re-read it in it's past tense!
Envision an end to this fear & it's influence over you.

You can burn it - even delete it!
(if it is on your electronic of choice)
or ...
Visualize it vaporize & disappear into thin air!

Then shower & wash it off -
wash off all the residue it left behind!

Its that simple if you choose it to be 

If for any reason triggers show up in your future...
Repeat the same exercise with the trigger as your subject.

& abracadabra it out of your mind & life!

Then simply wash it off!!!

& then celebrate your freeing of feelings
that you can now replace with great words ...
better feelings - with the better emotions attached!

Turning that fearing in your mind -
into **freeing of the mind** is your choice ❣

It's much like cleaning out the closet -
making room for new to come in!

When you clean up your mind storage...
You make room for new experiences :0)

What new experiences are you ready for?

Why don't you write of the new experiences you wish to welcome in...?
In present tense only of course! (like it exists in the now)
Use your senses to describe in great emotional detail -
the beauty of it all - enjoy it! Then re-read it!

While we lovely humans talk a lot of the future...
Writing in future tense means - it can never be in your now!!!

So get day dreaming in your now & feel all those wonderful feelings -
here & now!!!

As for your past,
your present & your future!
Wave good-bye to your past -
only retaining the best memories to cherish!
Engage in your present like the gift that it is -
living as you wish to & for your Greatest Good!
Look ahead into the future & all the possibilities -
as it becomes your here & now!!!

To dream right - you must dream big
& trust the process in the now!

Past, Present Or Future!

Where are you?

Are you living in your past, your present or your future?!

Wherever you may be - you have emotions attached!

What we focus on - will always expand!!!

So ask yourself ...

Are you doing the best you can do for you?

Is it serving you?

Are you repeating the same habits while expecting different results?

Who is ailing you?

Who is helping you?

Are you helping you?

Or is the hard truth...

You are not serving you?

Do you want to & Do you need to?

What do you truly need - to live a good life for you?

Truth is we need much less than the whims & wants ...

We habitually stress ourselves for!

If you are living in the past ...
you cannot know where you stand in the now ...
& so how would you expect - to be able to day dream your future into becoming your now?

The past is done! (It is behind you!)
There is a reason the rearview mirror is so small in a vehicle -
it is meant for glancing!
Like Glancing into your past memories for reference
of lessons learned or joyful memories...
being the only viewing of benefit - true?

eg: I used to ....

Your Present - (often referred to as the gift!)
It is your now!
You can only do in your now!
You can prepare & make steps for a future goal...
but you cannot live in the future -
there is only now!
Your mindful imagination is your tool of the now!

eg: I am ....

Your future - (your vision is now)
When you plan in future tense -
It can never exist in your now - true?
There is nothing wrong with planning a goal
with a future timeline -
by doing so you are saying you expect it in your
now on such & such date!

eg: I will be ....

So, if we learn by repetition - then would you not agree...
that the 'old fashioned' **LINES** ...
the many, many lines - the we once received in schools as a punishment -
to be so greatly beneficial today - possibly!?

THINK ABOUT THAT FOR A MOMENT!

When 1st learning the alphabet we did each letter repeatedly - true?
When learning a word - we found ways to repeat it...
over & over & over again! - true?

So why wouldn't we adopt this our whole life through -
but with a positive alignment?

Personally, I think it's the best!
Why?

Because...
we have to think about what we are writing, as we speak it to ourselves
& we also get to practice the penmanship too!
Penmanship is lacking in todays lifestyle wouldn't you agree? (BRING IT BACK!)

So instead of writing & repeating what you won't do anymore because...
you are not in teacher trouble.
Write & repeat - what it is you do want & will be doing in present tense!

Remembering - what we focus on - we get more of as long as your
emotionally invested & connected, to that which you want ...
like its already done!

Remembering too - that your new chapter...
is the new reason to be ready for this season
& the next! & the next! & the next!

Line writing examples

Today I get to choose to be … happy, joyful, understanding, helpful!!!!
Because - it is my choice! OR choose your own ending to the Because.

Today I get to feel … great, amazing, full of energy!!!
Because - I do wellness! OR / … & …

I am the best … daughter, co-worker, photographer, educator, etc!!!
Because - I am Brilliant! OR … & …

I am beautiful!
Because I see & feel how wonderful I am always! OR … & …

I am 'Greatful' for… my parents, my love / partner, my job,
my food etc!!!!
Because …I Appreciate all that I am becoming!
Because I am blossoming beautifully / evolving wonderfully / I
understand who I am, as I find Joy in something every day!
OR… & …

I Appreciate … feeling so amazing, so in tune with who I am!!
Because… & …

Go on - list all the those qualities you are & evolving into - in present time!

You are Amazing - so reach for your Amazing Authentic Self
& feel the Joy of you, as you navigate the rollercoaster of life -
experiencing great moments of Joy.

It doesn't matter who you are to someone else -
if you don't matter to you 1st!

REPEAT! REPEAT! REPEAT!

See it!   Hear it!   Smell it!   Taste it!   Touch it!

All that you want - and all in your minds eye!

Believe you already have it!

Have faith!

If there is even an inkling of doubt - your not all in yet!

Commitment to self & your thoughts … are priceless - NO?

You can get there - YES?

YES YOU CAN 💕

YOU CAN SEE IT, HEAR IT, SMELL IT, TASTE IT, TOUCH IT!

REPEAT REPEAT REPEAT💕💕💕

Happy repeating commitment to self💗

AGAIN, AGAIN & AGAIN!

Remember your brain doesn't know the difference between what's real & what is in your imagination! It hears it all!

Use it to your benefit ❣️

What is your **Memory** bank doing for you?

Would you agree its a record of the past?
Your personal library - true?

We all experience good & not so good memories ...
sometimes bad, really bad ...
even difficult situations - that are held in our memory bank - true?

This memory bank can be much like the Trash Can -
that we automatically throw things into.
& because the mind focuses 2 1/2 times more on the negative ...
there are many negative experiences that your memory bank holds.

If you choose, you can simply decide what things in that memory bank
are worth keeping there (active / some semi active)...
it is your choice - correct?

The memory is activated through our senses of ...
Feeling, Hearing, Seeing, Smelling, Tasting, Touching!
An experience of something that triggers a familiarity - true?.

You - yes you & only you can choose ...
what is worth keeping & what is worth deleting ...
because you are ultimately in charge of you - do you agree?

You get to decide what you want to delete ...
by seeing in your imagination - that memory **you -** throw into that trash can
& then choose to hit that delete button -
which permanently deletes it.
(You do it on your electronic of choice all the time!)
It is your choice to catch a thought & decide to think it further or
that it does not serve you - true?

Many of you are not '**a letting go**' type ...
If this be your truth - then the virtual storage pantry
might be your best go to tool.

This virtual pantry has big glass jars with stainless steel sealing lids ...
this pantry can hold as many jars as you see fit for you -
& labelled as you wish.

If a memory is no longer serving you ...
but you do feel that strong attachment of familiar feeling to it ...
the one that makes you feel unwilling to let go right now...
or, simply unable to deal with it at this present time...
you can simply ... virtually toss it into a jar of your choosing!
(possibly labelled 'no longer serves me')
& choose to pick it up or not at any later date of your choosing.

Meanwhile it is in safe keeping from interrupting your positive & present
mindset - if you decide to make this your choice!

My virtual pantry has many things in it to deal with later!

It's just like hanging your troubles as the door before you enter your job -
your work requires a trouble free focus mind - true?!
Just as some of us that need to hang the work stresses at the door -
before entering back home.

An actual jar is also good - if that is of your choosing -
to write it (your trouble or stress) & drop it in closing the lid.

In rough times -
Imagine you have a heart shaped glass bowl full of heart shaped rocks in it.
These rocks you can pick up & touch to appreciate something - to be
'**greatful**' or just as a reminder of the love it represents -
the love that you are.
You will soon see hearts everywhere! With the love they represent.
Your life is waiting to show you positive love ❣

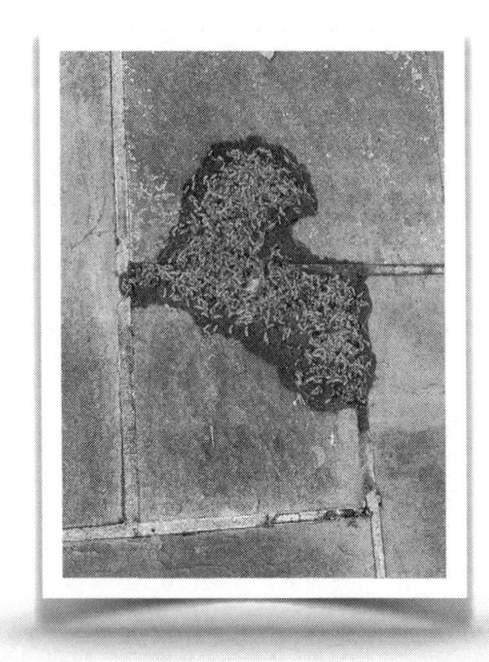

Are you Evolving or revolving?

Is it time you stop reacting in the same old way that irritates you...
& start **creating** ... that which can serve you for your greatest good?

If you are creating - you are quite possibly evolving - true?

If you are irritated - then it is likely you are involved in a pattern of your own or someone else's mess which does not align with you evolving - since you are possibly revolving!

You don't need to clarify the why's - as we get irritated by so many things in the reality of living this life - you just need to recognize that an irritation is present - in order to change the current (the now) feeling.

If it irritates you - it is not serving you - is it?

The choices to be 'irritated by' are many - true?

So just ask yourself - is it a revolving irritating issue?
or
Is it an unfamiliar Evolving journey?

You decide this for you!

If you have to argue for the limits a revolving issue presents...

Ask yourself - are you looking for reasons to stay with your familiar past
or
are you avoiding being in your present - as you look at the person in the mirror?

So what will you choose - to revolve or Evolve?
What do you see in your **reflection** in the mirror - is it an exact mirroring?

Are you looking at you & all the great qualities you possess?
or ... Are you looking & comparing yourself to someone
or something outside of yourself?

When you compare yourself to another - you are stealing your own joy!
Because - no 2 people or lives are exactly alike -
this is the beauty of the HUMAN RACE ❣ DIVERSITY AT ITS BEST ❣

Why not sit with yourself ... in front of your mirror -
gazing only into your eyes for about 20 mins or so.

As your eyes wander & they will - reset & go back to your eyes.
See them twinkle & sparkle in their beautiful color (s).

As your thoughts wander & they will again - reset & take your eyes back to the eyes reflecting back at you.

Feel every emotion as it rises & let it flow!
If it is negative ... say bye & let it float on by - then reset!

If it is positive ... add all those seeing, feeling descriptive words to your positive thought, for as long as you can & enjoy the magic of
the eyes you see that represent who you are.

It is said that our eyes are the windows to our soul...
So ... get to know that soul in present time with love
& the much needed undivided attention from your you - in your now ❣

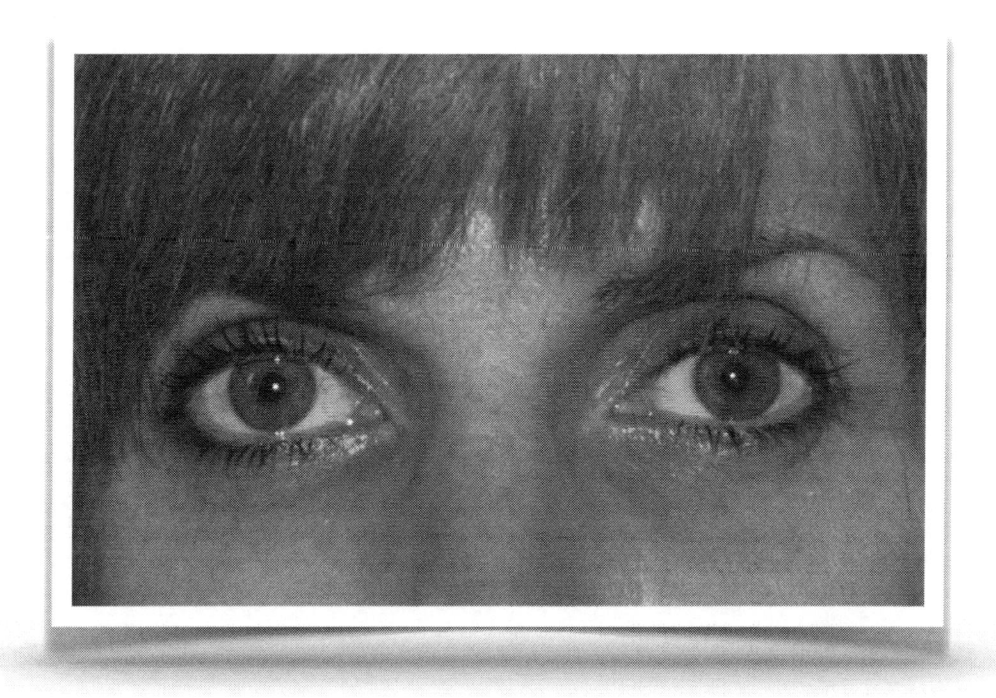

This tree reflection photo is credited to my young friend
Angel Gabriel Rivera Maldonado
Ocala, FL

What **Echoes** back at you consistently?
IS IT NEGATIVE OR POSITIVE?

If Negative - what do you believe the message is?
Is it a message that you have been ignoring?
Is it time to pay attention to the echoing?

If Positive - are you navigating that echo consistently?
or have you disregarded it...
to place your attention elsewhere?

To someone else's echo - possibly?

Are you echoing someone else?

What we see is most often what we do?
So what are you doing & why?

What do you want to echo & why?

Your choices are many - true?
To help narrow your choices...
Think of which choices will feel good to you ...
& echo that good to those around you!
Not a feeling of superior - but of the good & kind!
READ THAT AGAIN MY BUSY FRIEND ❕

Those who need to search for more of the superior feeling echoes...
can only do so by having someone else feel less than them!
Being neither good or kind - true?

Again I ask - What kind of Echo suits you & Why...
& is it for the Greatest Good of you, yours, one & all?

What Is Excellence To You?

It is usually related to a positive form of being...
at someone, something or other - correct?

But is it not true, that we are mostly excellent in negative things too?

It's definition describes being good - even outstanding = Excellence!

Are we not excellent at stress inducing ourselves...
into a cycle of feeling out of control?

Do you even understand that if you can be excellent
at negative behavior patterns ...
then - you can also be excellent at positive behavior patterns?

IT IS A CHOICE! - you can learn how to catch the negative &
change them into positive for your own benefit.
Which would you rather choose - Negative or Positive?

Is it that ... we are out of practice at consciously choosing, refocusing &
refining?

It really depends on what you accept & choose ...
to let influence your choosing & your focus - correct?

You can choose & focus positively always ... if you just pause -
review & refine your choices.

Choosing your attitude along with your action or reaction
is good choosing of your focus - NO?
Choosing & focusing well will always serve you well!

READ THAT AGAIN MY BUSY FRIEND!

Enthusiasm

Are you enthusiastic in all things ... that you do for your greatest good or just part time?

Can you decide to find some enthusiasm in most things you choose to do?
When we are enthusiastic - we feel strongly about that which we are focused upon - true?

So what ignites the enthusiasm in you? & Why?

When you feel enthusiastic - you are experiencing a form of passion - true?

Can you choose to be passionate about something that is to your benefit?

Do you believe only good things come to you through hard work...
the hard work that you do not feel enthusiastic, passionate or excited about?
WHY?

Who told you all good things come from struggle, hardship or needing to do this, that, or the other ... that of which you truly wish to never do?
If you believe this - it is true & can only be true for you!

If you choose to believe you can enjoy being passionately enthusiastic while gaining momentum in excitement - this will be true for you too!
So which would you rather choose to believe?

All new things feel like big deals - true?

But is it not true ... that even thinking about 1 small step into the direction of passion & enthusiasm is sparking the possibilities of excitement & Joy?

So What have you got to lose my busy friend?
What do you choose for you & why?

P	-	Personally
A	-	Accessing
S	-	Self
S	-	Sufficient
I	-	I
O	-	Over
N	-	Negative

Given that the **earth** is round ...
with so many growing trees all over our world...
Could it be that - the roots of trees help keep the earth bound together -
& Naturally so with gravity?

Would you agree our world is safer & cleaner with the trees in it?
Then why are we taking so many of them out ...
leaving our neighborhoods without -
that which - is more purifying to the air we breath?

Why are we so surprised when the earth beneath us or around us
& our homes gives way?
Why do you think flash flooding is as bad as it is? (just global warming?)
Would the trees, wild shrubs & wild flowers (often known as weeds)
use this excess water naturally?
All growth in nature has a rhyme & reason - no? **Something to ponder!**

If a tree can be related to our life - our roots & our growth...
it also holds our earth & life together ...
making homes for the native wildlife,
& keeping our air clean, etc. etc!

Then ... why are we destroying them so much?
When we destroy them - are we not destroying ourselves...
& the quality of life we are always in need of?
Hmmm!

Millions are spent on wanting to know & view other planets - true?
Why are we not prioritizing the helping of the planet we live on in present time?
One would think this be a priority - no?
Millions are spent on preventing extinctions of all kinds - true?
Yet - the millions are still being spent on destruction of the nature they once thrived in. READ THAT AGAIN MY BUSY FRIEND

THE ABUSE OF THE PLANET WE WANT TO THRIVE IN - IS UNREAL!
WE ARE NOT ALLOWING THE PLANET TO THRIVE NATURALLY IT SEEMS!

WHY - ARE WE NOT THINKING BEYOND OURSELVES (to help ourselves)
& OF THE WANTS, NEEDS, NECESSARIES & DESIRES THAT ARE & FOR
THE GREATEST GOOD?

WHAT IS ACTUALLY NECESSARY?

I WOULD HIGHLY RECOMMEND **WATCHING** ...
BEFORE THE FLOOD
& **KISS THE GROUND** -
ENLIGHTENING ON SO MANY LEVELS!

As for the news -
you cannot change what is true news -
but the news - sure can change you!
So make it a choice on what you let in!

I prefer to watch **CBS New York**
with **Gail King, Tony Dukoupil** & **Nate Burleson** -
along with their extended crew.
They cover the news without the heightened exaggeration.
They do not get enthusiastically excited when reporting the negative.
They **focus & get enthusiastic on the feel good news** -
along with a small segment called the **UPLIFT & so much more**❣

Who of you - are choosing to listen to a station or channel because ...
it has a positive style over the dramatics spun on negativity?

What are you choosing & / or not choosing to let in?

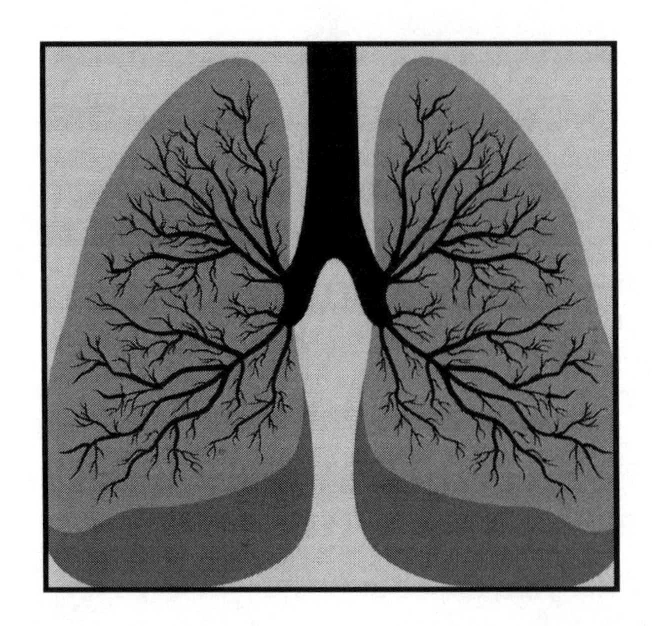

Would you believe when looking at a diagram of the lungs - it resembles a tree?

Very much like a tree - true?

The tree helps keep the air clean enough for us to breath - true?

Do you take your breath for granted since it is done -
so automatically, without any thought about it?
We mostly do!!!

How about treating yourself to a few moments in nature...
(if your able - otherwise in your mindful imagination)
Enjoy your senses - as they tell you all you see, hear, feel, taste & touch!

Breath intentionally - with purpose / on purpose & be 'greatful' for the ability to enjoy & breath!

Take that breath & feel your lungs fill - hold it for a moment ...
& know that oxygen filters through into your body (imagine this)
& breath out!
It's called exercising your lungs - your lungs look after you - true?
Isn' it about time you took care of them too?

Appreciation goes a long way in how our wellness translates - true?
So - can you appreciate a diagram comparison of a tree stump & thumb print?

Interesting Fact :

The inner of the tree pattern is as unique as your thumb print.
It is amazing how alike they actually look?

How amazing is the Divine that we get to enjoy ...
all that has been created for us
to use to our benefit?

What can you divinely appreciate?

IGNITE YOUR SPARK

Wake up & light your spark 

Dress up & light your spark

Change up your routine & light your spark 

Play your favorite tunes & light your spark 

Dance like no one is watching & light your spark 

Just light your spark

in all the best ways ...

Until ...

your spark turns into

full on joy

To enjoy

My hope is that you have had some mini revelations, new sparks of joy & amazing possibilities firing up inside your heart & mindful imagination as you travelled your path through the many questions.

You have a choice to suffer the past or stress the future in your memory & / or imagination only - these are the only ways they can exist in your now!

Your choice is to decide what your new **'in the now'** sparks are to be ... or to keep reigniting old ones that cannot & / or do not serve you & your greatest good!

HAPPY CHOOSING & USING YOUR MINDFUL IMAGINATION FOR ...
YOUR GREATEST GOOD MY BUSY 🐝 FRIEND ❣

Healthy Limits & Boundaries = Love of Self & Those Around You!
It's time to re-challenge yourself in this exercise :0)

Again - It would also be wise of you - if you can describe from an emotional standpoint - as you think of these limits & boundaries.

1/
My emotions around this are....

2/
My emotions around this are....

3/
My emotions around this are....

4/
My emotions around this are....

5/
My emotions around this are....

6/
My emotions around this are....

7/
My emotions around this are....

This concludes our 1st reading of this small journey together of

Write a note to self ...

in appreciation of your you - your WithIn!

& Remember....

What you desire - desires you - if true!

Know - that you hold all the answers **within!**

Love of self, those that surround you &

the world as a whole can only influence **your super power**

if you choose!

Finding your **key** - is the unlocking of the

doorway **to the hero within you**!

Love is the master key that opens the gates of happiness!

A KINDNESS - TO SELF!

A - A

K - Knowing

I - Inside

N - Never

D - Dies / Denies

N - New

E - Experiences

S - Satisfy (ing)

S - Self

Yes - Everything Counts, So - Be Thankful

What are you thankful for?

When one door closes - there is always a new door waiting to be unlocked or a frame of time & opportunity showing itself... for your choosing!

The ability of possibilities you possess are endless❣

MY INTENTION - I MENTION -

THAT BELIEVIN' IS RECEIVING!

WITH LOVE FROM THE DIVINE!

With my Intention I mention
What my action & my reaction
What my truth is to be
Because believin' is receiving
In it's greatest form!

My intention is true
As I mention it to you
& for the world to hear
That I expect to do better - for you my honey better
Even greater when it's later
Because believin' is receiving
In it's greatest form!

I mention my action
As I promise to you - the beautiful wonderful you!
The intention I'm setting
Is a truth I hold true
As my action
Brings the reaction
Of a great memory in motion
Because Believin' is receiving
In the motion of our ocean
In it's greatest form

My truth I can see
As it slowly but surely
Comes in forward focus
Of life's meaning to me
& of my honey babe
How great it is to see
That you my love babe
Are really seeing me
The truth of who I am
That I was always meant to be
Because believin' is receiving
In it's greatest form

To Love me is to see me
In my shadows & my light
With all the love I hold for you
That really shines both glowing & so bright
To be with me is to hear me
For all I have to say
Cos saying how much I Love You
Will never get old each day
For I'm no longer just a mention
without the full Intention
Because believin' is receiving
in its greatest form.

It's time we live, love & laugh
As much as we both can
Tomorrows are never promised
In This relationship Of Life
So - I want to live, love & laugh with you
Cos' this Joy is all we need
To be seen & to be heard
is the greatest Joy indeed
Because Believin' is receiving
In it's greatest form

Now we are Living, Loving & Laughing
Beyond our every thought
As yesterdays Tomorrows
Become our best todays
Each Tomorrow & Today
That comes, goes & flows
Will build upon the forever lasting
Life that is yet to be told!

By De L
May 2023

In conclusion my busy friends…

Your buried treasure is <u>WITH</u> you - It is <u>IN</u> you 

You started this reading maybe feeling a little dull & unpolished inside …
You have now chosen to look <u>within</u> - absorb & or do the thought &
written exercises that are & / or feel beneficial to you …
in your present life circumstances.
There is no doubt - you are a shiny colorful gem who is open to self
growth, life elevation & willing to understand that
energy is everything…
<u>with a clearer understanding of where your attention goes your energy
flows</u>

APPRECIATION comes from the heart & can be found in all things
Exercise your heart with all it can appreciate & feel all its vibrations
Then relax & think positively - while being aware of what is possible
Feel what shines bright for you - you amazing honey Soul

Understand if you ever feel boredom - you are in a perfect place to give
birth to creation - beginning & ending with your choice of thoughts.
Find your focus & reach for that content enthusiasm, that can quickly
evolve into a passion inducing empowerment!
Appreciate your freedom to choose
as you come from a place of **love** -
on **your journey of joy** to a destination
that had began in your mind.

Remember **Joy** is not only
at your desired destination -
it **is on your Journey**

When you can say you have enjoyed your journey however big or small - you have arrived at your WITHIN

W - Why

I - Is

T - The

H - Heart

I - In

N - Now

THERE IS ONLY NOW!

With Grace you can plan or plant

&

grow your own new tree of life -

whenever you choose

Fun Facts :

Sunflowers help clean up contaminated soil ❣️
They lovingly detoxify - absorbing heavy metals ❣️
They also boost the immune system of the bumble 🐝
& honey 🐝🐝🐝
So - do your part & plant with intention to help the bees, butterflies & pollinators of our beautiful planet ❣️
They represent faith, happiness, hope & unity
as well as a connection of the higher power ❣️

This photo is credited to my friend Gail Purdy-Cypherd Fishers Island, NY

You my busy friend
have the power WITH-IN
to evolve as far as you wish
in vibration
to experience
all there is available to you

Remember only you can limit you 
You have the Freedom to Choose

So what do you choose
for you
in this human experience
for the greatest good

Restore your you / your WITHIN -
with self love & appreciation!
Then grow your own inner tree my honey friend

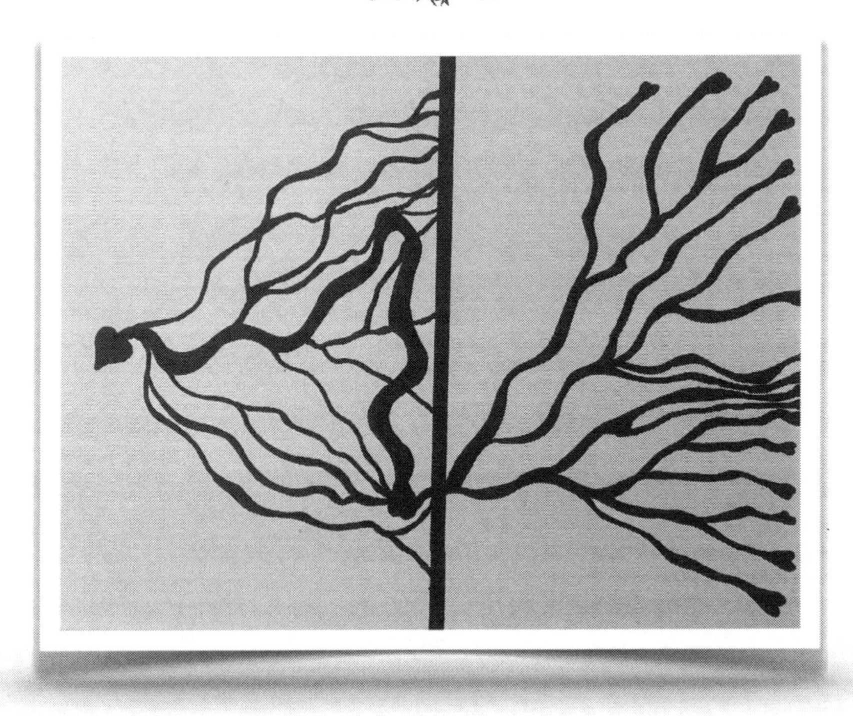

/|\

LEFT - the heavy path to date | RIGHT - your future path choices

YOU TODAY

Your Perception is everything - it shapes your world 

My vision for you - is to be authentically you
Be your unique brave self, with nothing but love for your own soul…
& those you encounter in your lifes' journey

I hope your journey throughout this book brought you closer
& more connected than ever - to your inner authentic self…
that believes in you wholeheartedly

To **Dream right** - you must dream big **in your now** …
knowing **you are worthy** of all your desires.
May **your joy** be plentiful in your lifes' **journey** -
with **your authentic ethical** self **honesty …**
being a part of your make up **going forward**

For those who bring your **attention** to negativity -
may you **kindly -** yet **politely** steer them to the positive side of your
street (so to speak) **or** kindly leave them in your rearview mirror!
Remember - what you resist will always persist - READ THAT AGAIN

May you forever see there is a **silver lining** in all of your lifes' **experiences**
as you experience being a special part **of the human race.**

WE ARE ALL ONE RACE - FROM THE SAME ENERGY SOURCE

We are each that mustard seed of the Dear Divine
You are the miracle you have been searching for

GIVE **G**ENEROUSLY

GIVE **R**ESPECTFULLY

GIVE **A**CTION

GIVE **C**OMPASSIONATELY

GIVE **E**NERGY

GRACE – WILL ALWAYS SERVE YOU WELL ❣

Printed in Great Britain
by Amazon